BUSINESS CONTINUITY MANAGEMENT SYSTEMS

BCS, THE CHARTERED INSTITUTE FOR IT

Our mission as BCS, The Chartered Institute for IT, is to enable the information society. We promote wider social and economic progress through the advancement of information technology science and practice. We bring together industry, academics, practitioners and government to share knowledge, promote new thinking, inform the design of new curricula, shape public policy and inform the public.

Our vision is to be a world-class organisation for IT. Our 70,000 strong membership includes practitioners, businesses, academics and students in the UK and internationally. We deliver a range of professional development tools for practitioners and employees. A leading IT qualification body, we offer a range of widely recognised qualifications.

Further Information
BCS, The Chartered Institute for IT,
First Floor, Block D,
North Star House, North Star Avenue,
Swindon, SN2 1FA, United Kingdom.
T +44 (0) 1793 417 424
F +44 (0) 1793 417 444
www.bcs.org/contact

BUSINESS CONTINUITY MANAGEMENT SYSTEMS
Implementation and certification to ISO 22301

Hilary Estall

Published by BCS Learning & Development Ltd, a wholly owned subsidiary of BCS The Chartered Institute for IT, First Floor, Block D, North Star House, North Star Avenue, Swindon, SN2 1FA, UK.
www.bcs.org

ISBN: 978-1-78017-146-3
PDF ISBN: 978-1-78017-147-0
ePUB ISBN: 978-1-78017-148-7
Kindle ISBN: 978-1-78017-149-4

British Cataloguing in Publication Data.
A CIP catalogue record for this book is available at the British Library.

Typeset by Lapiz Digital Services, Chennai, India.
Printed and bound by CPI Group (UK) Ltd, Croydon, CR0 4Y.

CONTENTS

LIST OF FIGURES AND TABLES

AUTHOR

Hilary Estall SBCI is a respected authority on management system standards. Working for a leading certification body for more than 11 years and directly responsible for the development of its business continuity management system auditing scheme, Hilary has amassed extensive experience since the publication of BS 25999-2 in 2007.

Hilary is a member of the British Standards Institution (BSI) Technical Standards Committee BCM/1 and plays an active part in the ongoing maintenance of BS 25999 Parts 1 and 2. In addition, as part of this committee, Hilary has reviewed and commented on ISO 22301 and ISO 22313 during the course of their respective development stages.

Now running her own successful business continuity consultancy firm, Perpetual Solutions Limited (www.pslinfo.co.uk), Hilary works with a variety of clients supporting them through the different stages of business continuity management system implementation, certification and maintenance. Hilary is an IRCA (International Register of Certificated Auditors) registered BCMS (business continuity management system) Lead Auditor and also continues to provide auditing services on behalf of a number of certification bodies, thus enabling her to maintain her professional qualification with the International Register of Certificated Auditors.

FOREWORD

The International Standard for Business Continuity – ISO 22301 – is now officially released and it comes at a time when the need for good BCM (business continuity management) practice has never been greater.

The new standard has been developed in collaboration with experts from around the world to ensure its international relevance and applicability, and to ensure it meets the needs of global organisations. It is hoped that the new standard will create a path for greater international consistency, and encourage worldwide adoption of good BCM practice by organisations of all sizes and in all sectors. Building on the existing work of National Standard bodies in a number of countries, most significantly the work done in the UK by the British Standards Institution, ISO 22301 provides an improved framework of good practice and a common language to help organisations with operational activities in multiple countries to better compare business continuity (BC) needs and capabilities globally.

Furthermore, ISO 22301 offers new clarity about the responsibilities of senior management in BC as well as on the role of BC in risk mitigation and disaster avoidance. It demonstrates the need for a balanced relationship between risk management and BC.

Because BC is spread across an entire organisation, it is particularly suitable for a formal management systems approach. This provides a consistent means of measuring the effectiveness of an organisation's BCM programme and how well it is embedded into its culture and business priorities. Certification against ISO 22301 will demonstrate the importance placed on BC by senior management.

Similar management systems are used for other disciplines, such as information security (ISO 27001) and quality (ISO 9001), so this allows organisations to converge around the common framework known as 'Plan, Do, Check, Act'. ISO 22301 is also spearheading the drive towards a consistent documentation framework for ISO Management Systems standards as defined in ISO Guide 83.

We have come a long way since the first mention of BC in a management systems standard, in its debut as a single section in the Information Security standard BS 7799 (which rapidly became ISO 17799), nearly two decades ago. The growing BC community was less than satisfied with that positioning and actively promoted the idea of a BCM standard in its own right. The early attempt at this was PAS 56, which was released to mixed reaction but nevertheless did encourage professionals around the world to give serious thought to what BCM really was and how it could be properly described and codified. The period from 2005 onwards has been a productive one for those wishing to construct BCM standards with much work undertaken at both national and international levels.

Although a positive development for the growth of the subject, it has had a downside in terms of the take-up of formal standards by organisations that were becoming increasingly confused by the myriad of terms and standards that were circulating. ISO 22301 has been a long time coming and we all hope that it will end the uncertainty felt in recent years by many practitioners about the future role and positioning of BCM in their organisations. One of the most important factors of its success will be its take-up by organisations, and that will largely depend upon the clarity in which its purpose and practical value is communicated. It is in this context that the book by Hilary Estall is very important. I have known Hilary since the early years of developing BS 25999 when she was directly responsible for how the emerging standard should be audited. We did not always agree, practitioners and auditors do not necessarily see things from the same standpoint, but I always respected her views and hopefully that was mutual. In fact, she must have found the subject as interesting as I do because she now runs a highly respected professional BCM consultancy firm herself.

Reflecting on this book, it seemed to me that Hilary has an almost unique set of skills which enabled her to write it. She understands audit, she understands business continuity and she knows how to put the two together, thus maximising the value of the discipline to an organisation. I was particularly struck by her observation that 'when implementing a BCMS, management system requirements and BCM requirements are equally important'. This is great advice. BCM is not just compliance or a tick-box exercise but neither is it a free for all for BCM practitioners to indulge their theories. Curiously enough, nearly 20 years ago my (and now Hilary's) institute, The Business Continuity Institute, coined the term The Art and Science of BCM. Little did we know then how well that phrase describes the conflicting needs for imaginative BCM solutions to be balanced within a measurable consistent process and framework.

If you just want to know more about ISO 22301, I suggest this is the first (and perhaps only) book you need to read. If you are going further and want to become an ISO 22301 certified company then it gives you the route, the dangers, the tips and the confidence to succeed. Enjoy reading it, even if you previously thought BCMS was a dry subject, you might well be very surprised.

Lyndon Bird FBCI
Technical Development Director at the Business Continuity Institute (www.thebci.org).

ACKNOWLEDGEMENTS

Writing articles for various business continuity journals and websites gave me the courage to develop my writing skills so when asked if I had ever thought of writing a book the idea was slightly less daunting than it might otherwise have been. Nevertheless, I would not have been able to complete this book without the input and support of Simon, Emma and David, all of whom have used their practical knowledge of business continuity management systems to provide steerage when I might otherwise have run off course.

Finally, I could not have written this book without the love and encouragement of my husband, Clive. His belief in me has kept me focused and committed to see it through to the end.

Permission to reproduce extracts from ISO 22301:2012, ISO 9000:2005, PAS 99:2006, ISO 19011:2011 and BS 25999-1:2006 is granted by BSI. British Standards can be obtained in PDF or hard copy formats from the BSI online shop: www.bsigroup.com/Shop or by contacting BSI Customer Services for hardcopies only: Tel: +44 (0)20 8996 9001, Email: cservices@bsigroup.com.

ABBREVIATIONS

BC	Business continuity
BCI	Business Continuity Institute
BCM	Business continuity management
BCMS	Business continuity management system
BIA	Business impact analysis
BSI	The British Standards Institution
IRCA	International Register of Certificated Auditors
MTPD	Maximum tolerable period of disruption
PDCA	Plan Do Check Act
RTO	Recovery time objective
UKAS	United Kingdom Accreditation Service

1 INTRODUCTION

WHO SHOULD READ THIS BOOK?

Implementing a business continuity management system (BCMS) requires commitment, time, resourcefulness and plenty of support from your management team. Whatever the drivers behind the journey you are about to embark on, you need to be well equipped to survive the ups and downs that will occur along the way. If you can answer 'yes' to any of the following statements, this book is written with you in mind and will provide you with practical and straight forward advice:

- Your organisation is seeking formal certification to ISO 22301.

- Your organisation is seeking alignment to ISO 22301.

- Your organisation is considering whether to become certified and wishes to understand what is involved before committing resource.

- Your organisation is working towards, or has already achieved, certification to BS 25999-2 and wishes to understand what is involved in moving from one standard to another.

- You wish to develop your own understanding of what is required to implement an effective BCMS.

- You are looking for a practical support mechanism to guide you through the implementation stages of your BCMS.

The need for this handbook became clear to me during my own personal journey through BCMSs. Auditing numerous BS 25999 management systems has shown me time and time again that there are three independent factions:

(1) Those who are existing BC professionals and are implementing a management system for the first time.

(2) Those who already have experience with implementing other management systems, but are new to BCM.

(3) Those who have no prior experience in either aspect.

I concluded that missing from the raft of technical publications already available is a practical guide that bridges the two subject areas and helps manage expectations along the way.

To emphasise the importance of particular BCMS requirements you will notice a degree of repetition in the book. This is intentional and will hopefully reinforce the messages!

THE OBJECTIVE OF THIS BOOK

Management systems, if not implemented properly, can be seen as the proverbial millstone around an organisation's neck. This book aims to focus on what is significant about management systems and how best to achieve intended results. By concentrating on what is most important, the organisation will enjoy the benefits of a management system which has been developed to meet **its** specific needs.

READER BEWARE!

This handbook is not aimed at providing you with detailed instructions on how to implement BCM. There are several publications that will offer you advice, for example, on how to undertake a business impact analysis, carry out a risk assessment or write a BC plan and you should refer to those if you are seeking that level of support.

HOW TO USE THIS BOOK

The aim of this handbook is that it becomes your BCMS best friend! It is a tool that should be used when required rather than read from cover to cover and then set aside.

It is set out in four parts. Two focus on management systems themselves and the certification process, and the remaining two look at BCM and the requirements of ISO 22301, translating them into user friendly guidance notes.

Checklists are available for you to self assess your progress with a particular requirement, and action sheets are included to encourage you to develop your BCMS as you progress through the handbook. **Do not be afraid to write in the space provided**. As you read, thoughts will come into your head. These initial thoughts will often prove to be the most important and you should capture them before they are lost.

You will find 'Top Tips' throughout the book, which may prove useful to you during your BCMS journey. These tips have been gathered from my own experience and individuals who have been involved in the audit process in some way. My thanks to all those who have contributed their great ideas. You know who you are!

I wish you well with your journey into business continuity management systems and hope this handbook provides the support and guidance that you are looking for in order to achieve your BCMS objectives.

2 MANAGEMENT SYSTEMS UNCOVERED

PURPOSE AND OBJECTIVE

The purpose of this chapter of the handbook is to explain what a management system is and its key components. We will look at how management systems have developed over time as well as consider planned developments for the future. You will learn that there are core requirements for every management system, including BCMSs.

The objective is to provide guidance and support to both those looking to implement a BCMS for the first time and those who wish to take this opportunity to review their existing system and consider how it may be improved.

TERMS AND DEFINITIONS

For the purposes of this chapter of the handbook, and the broader consideration of what makes up a management system, the definitions provided in ISO 22301:2012 apply unless otherwise stated.

Competence: ability to apply knowledge and skills to achieve intended results

Continual Improvement: recurring activity to enhance performance (Source: ISO 22300)

Corrective Action: action to eliminate the cause of a nonconformity and to prevent recurrence[1] (Source: ISO 22300)

Document: information and its supporting medium[2]

Effectiveness: extent to which planned activities are realised and planned results achieved (Source: ISO 22300)

---

[1] In the case of other undesirable outcomes, action is necessary to minimise or eliminate causes and to reduce impact or prevent recurrence. Such actions fall outside the concept of 'corrective action' in the sense of this definition.

[2] The medium can be paper, magnetic, electronic or optical computer disc, photograph or master sample, or a combination thereof. A set of documents, for example specifications and records, is frequently called 'documentation'.

Internal Audit: audit conducted by, or on behalf of, the organisation itself for management review and other internal purposes, and which might form the basis for an organisation's self declaration of conformity[3]

Management System: set of interrelated or interacting elements of an organisation to establish policies and objectives, and processes to achieve those objectives[4]

Nonconformity: non-fulfilment of a requirement (Source: ISO 22300)

Policy: intentions and direction of an organisation as formally expressed by its top management

Procedure: specified way to carry out an activity or a process[5] (Source: ISO 9000:2005)

Record: statement of results achieved or evidence of activities performed

Top Management: person or group of people who directs and controls an organisation at the highest level[6]

MANAGEMENT SYSTEMS EXPLAINED

In order to put management systems into context, we start with a brief look at how these systems came about. We will then take a more detailed look at the core requirements of a management system and provide you with a practical insight into the areas that require particular consideration. Everything written in this chapter is relevant to business continuity management systems and should be considered as part of your BCMS implementation programme.

Origins

Even if you have never been involved with management systems before, you have probably heard of BS 5750 or ISO 9001. BS 5750 was one of the first widely recognised quality management systems, introduced in 1979 and the forerunner to the better known and internationally applied ISO 9000 series of standards. The aim of these standards was to help organisations introduce consistent methods of delivering products and services in ways which would increase quality, accuracy

---

[3] In many cases, particularly in smaller organisations, independence can be demonstrated by the freedom from responsibility for the activity being audited.

[4] A management system can address a single discipline or several disciplines.
The system elements include the organisation's structure, roles and responsibilities, planning, operation etc.
The scope of a management system can include the whole of the organisation, specific and identified functions of the organisation, specific and identified sections of the organisation, or one or more functions across a group of organisations.

[5] Procedures can be documented or not.
When a procedure is documented, the term 'written procedure' or 'documented procedure' is frequently used. The document that contains a procedure can be called a 'procedure document'.

[6] Top management has the power to delegate authority and provide resources within the organisation.
If the scope of the management system covers only part of an organisation, then top management refers to those who direct and control that part of the organisation.

and efficiency. It was later generally recognised to increase an organisation's competitive edge.

Management principles

When the ISO 9000 standards were introduced, eight quality management principles were identified, which, when applied by top management, were perceived to help an organisation improve its performance.

1. Customer focus

Organisations depend on their customers and therefore should understand current and future customer needs, should meet customer requirements and strive to exceed customer expectations.

2. Leadership

Leaders establish unity of purpose and direction of the organisation. They should create and maintain the internal environment in which people can become fully involved in achieving the organisation's objectives.

3. Involvement of people

People at all levels are the essence of an organisation and their full involvement enables their abilities to be used for the organisation's benefit.

4. Process approach

A desired result is achieved more efficiently when activities and related resources are managed as a process.

5. System approach to management

Identifying, understanding and managing interrelated processes as a system contributes to the organisations effectiveness and efficiency in achieving its objectives.

6. Continual improvement

Continual improvement of the organisation's overall performance should be a permanent objective of the organisation.

7. Factual approach to decision making

Effective decisions are based on the analysis of data and information.

8. Mutually beneficial supplier relationships

An organisation and its suppliers are interdependent and a mutually beneficial relationship enhances the ability of both to create value.

(Source: BS EN ISO 9000:2005).

No doubt you will recognise at least some of these principles from reading documents, standards and specifications on the subject of BC, risk management and other related subjects. The ISO 22301 standard, *Societal Security – Business Continuity Management System – Requirements*, has been developed along the same lines, although some of the terminology may look different.

As mentioned above, and linked to the eight management principles, there are some common management system requirements. They are:

- The organisation shall document the scope of the management system and the management system standards/specifications to which it subscribes.

- The organisation shall establish, document, implement, maintain and continually improve the management system in accordance with the requirements of the management system standards/specifications to which it subscribes.

- In order to meet its declared policies and objectives, the organisation shall:

  o identify the processes needed for the implementation, operation and maintenance of the management system, and their application throughout the organisation;

  o determine the sequence and interaction of these processes and the applicability for integration of these processes;

  o determine criteria and methods needed to ensure that both the operation and control of these processes are effective;

  o ensure the availability of resources and information necessary to support the operation and monitoring of these processes;

  o monitor, measure and analyse these processes, and implement actions necessary to achieve planned results and continual improvement of the organisation's overall performance.

(Source: PAS 99:2006).

How management systems have evolved

Over the years, these principles and requirements have continued to evolve. Where BS 5750 was concerned with compliance, over time, and through the ISO 9001 version updates, this has been superseded with a more cohesive approach towards continual improvement and the overall effectiveness of the management system. Conformance is no longer seen as enough; added value from a management system is now required by its users.

At the time this book went to print, a specially convened ISO Committee was looking at how management systems may be better aligned in order for the high level structure and common requirements to be systematically applied to future management system standards. This will assist organisations which have, or are looking to, introduce more than one management system as well as encourage a more standardised approach to implementing different management systems generally.

Two part management systems

Management systems invariably come in two parts;

(1) Structural requirements

(2) Technical requirements specific to individual standards.

In this section we will turn our attention specifically to BCMSs.

Business Continuity Management (BCM): holistic management process that identifies potential threats to an organisation and the impacts to business operations those threats, if realised, might cause, and which provides a framework for building organisational resilience with the capability of an effective response that safeguards the interests of its key stakeholders, reputation, brand and value-creating activities.

Business Continuity Management Systems (BCMS): part of the overall management system that establishes, implements, operates, monitors, reviews, maintains and improves business continuity[7].

In my experience, disproportionate levels of attention are often placed on these two aspects of BCMS requirements, and which comes through as the stronger element will depend on who has been given responsibility for implementing the system and their professional background. Where possible, a team approach should be considered, in order to draw upon different areas of knowledge.

TOP TIP

When implementing a BCMS, management system requirements and BCM requirements are equally important. Do not assume otherwise and lose sight of one of these two aspects of your BCMS. You are unlikely to achieve certification unless both elements are fully implemented and effective.

Keeping your management system 'local'

Whilst international standards are written by committees comprising several member countries, you should never lose sight of the fact that your management system must reflect the needs of **your** organisation. The requirements are written in such a way to be applicable across companies of different sizes, whether based in a single country or multiple countries across the globe. However, for those readers who work in a multinational organisation, you will know that cultural differences exist and need to be respected. It is very important that these local practices and expectations are managed with consideration, and for procedures to reflect these regional variations. This extends to your management system and how you set about demonstrating local application. Remember, if you are to be audited by an external company, it is their responsibility to understand where cultural differences may exist and tailor their expectations accordingly.

TOP TIP

Find an approach which works well with your organisation's culture whilst also complying with the requirements of the standard. In other words, make your BCMS fit around your business and not the other way round.

---

[7] The management system includes organisational structure, policies, planning activities, responsibilities, procedures, processes and resources. Source: ISO 22301:2012.

ACTION SHEET

To help support your organisation's decision to implement a BCMS, create a summary of the benefits of adopting ISO 22301 in order to help focus peoples' minds and management commitment.

PLAN DO CHECK ACT (PDCA) MODEL

As with all management systems, BCMSs follow a recognised and methodical approach to improving processes. It is known as the PDCA model[8] and, through a series of actions, encourages the continual improvement of the processes captured within the scope of the system. The PDCA model is often depicted at the start of the management system standard and ISO 22301 is no exception. Figure 2.1 illustrates how the PDCA model is applied to BCMS processes and Table 2.1 provides explanatory notes for each of the PDCA elements.

---

[8] PDCA model was originally based on the work of Walter Shewhart who pioneered statistical process control in the 1930s and which W Edwards Deming subsequently developed into the continual improvement or Deming cycle.

Figure 2.1 Application of PDCA model to BCMS processes

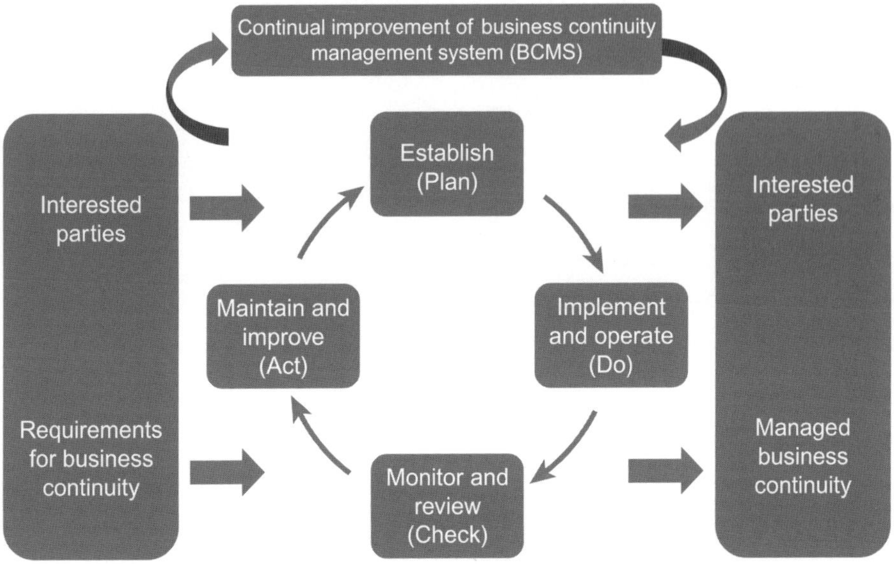

(Source: ISO 22301:2012)

Table 2.1 The PDCA elements

Plan (Establish)	Establish BC policy, objectives, targets, controls, processes and procedures relevant to improving BC in order to deliver results that align with the organisation's overall policies and objectives.
Do (Implement and operate)	Implement and operate the BC policy, controls, processes and procedures.
Check (Monitor and review)	Monitor and review performance against BC policy and objectives, report the results to management for review, and determine and authorise actions for remediation and improvement.
Act (Maintain and improve)	Maintain and improve the BCMS by taking corrective action, based on the results of management review and reappraising the scope of the BCMS and business continuity policy and objectives.

Source: ISO 22301:2012.

MANDATORY REQUIREMENTS FOR MANAGEMENT SYSTEMS

Building on the eight management principals and common elements of management systems, there are mandatory requirements across all management system standards.

- Determining the scope of the management system;
- Top management responsibilities with respect to the management system;
- Management system documentation;
- Improvement;
- Writing policies and setting objectives;
- Allocation of suitable resources and determining competencies;
- Evaluation of the performance and effectiveness of the management system;
- Internal Audit;
- Management Review;
- Nonconformity and Corrective Action Review.

We will now look at each of these requirements in detail. All are relevant to BCMSs.

DETERMINING THE SCOPE OF THE MANAGEMENT SYSTEM

It stands to reason that until you have 'scoped' your management system, you cannot reasonably build it. In other words, until you have decided what will be included, and possibly excluded, you are not in a position to develop its core components.

Surprisingly, defining the scope of your system is not always the first item on the BCMS agenda, but it should be! Would a new company launch its business before it had decided what products or services it was going to sell? No. So, why would you start developing a management system when you do not know what it will include?

Focusing on BCMSs in particular, in Table 2.2 are some questions that you need to answer before developing your scope.

Table 2.2 Questions to ask before developing the BCMS scope

Question	Your Response
1. What is the organisation's main purpose and what are its key products and services?	
2. What does the organisation consider to be its requirements for BC? In other words, would it focus its efforts on maintaining **some** or **all** of its products and services?	
3. If some products and services were to be excluded from the scope, what would be the justification for this decision?	
4. What is the overarching business strategy of the organisation?	
5. Has the organisation considered what its level of risk acceptance is? If so, what is it and why?	
6. Who are the main interested parties (otherwise known as key stakeholders) of the business and what are their needs and expectations?	
7. What statutory, regulatory and contractual responsibilities does the organisation have?	

Table 2.3 Questions to ask to determine the most important products and services

Question	Your Response
1. What are your revenue streams for core and non-core product and service lines?	
2. How would losing the ability to offer certain products and services damage your reputation and image?	
3. Is the organisation obligated by specific legal, regulatory or contractual requirements on certain products, services and clients?	
4. Does the organisation depend on a single or few key clients?	
5. What contractual obligations does the organisation have to its key clients or suppliers?	
6. Are there particular competitors that might take advantage if certain products and services were unavailable from your organisation?	

Once you have answers to these questions, you are closer to being in a position to identify an appropriate scope for your BCMS.

To help you determine which of your products and services are most important to your organisation, you should consider the questions in Table 2.3

Exclusions
It is fine to exclude certain products or services, but you must document any exclusions. Exclusions, including any support functions, must not impact on the organisations' ability to provide BC as determined by the business impact analysis and risk assessment (more about this in Chapter 2). Legal and regulatory requirements must also be considered when deciding whether to exclude anything from the scope of your BCMS in order not to overlook a key requirement or obligation.

Having considered all of the above, you will be in a stronger position to identify a scope that truly reflects your business priorities. Whilst the focus should be on your key products and services, you must also consider what supporting business functions are required in order for the organisation to fulfil its commitments. This is likely to include, but is not limited to, IT and telecoms support, payroll, staff welfare support, facilities management and billing.

Whether your organisation chooses a scope that encompasses the entire business operation or only part of it will in part be determined by the size and complexity of the business. This is a decision for top management to make, based on the above factors. Whatever scope is identified, the important point is that it reflects the priorities of the business and its stakeholders and can be 'ring fenced' if it is not covering the entire business operation.

Examples of BCMS scopes
Table 2.4 should assist you in considering what to include:

Table 2.4 Acceptable and unacceptable scopes

Acceptable scopes	Unacceptable scopes
The provision of exam marking services	The provision of (internal) payroll services, i.e. to your own employees
The design and delivery of training courses	Internal administration support
The manufacture, packaging and distribution of XYZ products	Delivery of ABC' contract only (i.e. one of many contracts)

Extending your scope at a later date

It is possible to extend the scope of your BCMS over time. You may decide to restrict the scope initially to allow you to develop an effective system, learning from the challenges you experience along the way. Once you are confident that your system is fundamentally sound (and compliant if you are seeking certification to a standard), you can then introduce a more comprehensive scope. Some companies try to scope their BCMS too broadly and suffer as a result. Whilst the scope may be driven by customer requirements, it is sometimes better to start off small and expand gradually. You will be able to build on your success and continue to take staff with you on your BCMS journey, rather than lose them somewhere along the way if your vast BCMS scope collapses at the first hurdle.

If you are seeking certification of your extended BCMS, you will need to advise your certification body of the proposed new scope and explain if this involves additional locations and resource. This will need to be factored into their future audit programme and additional audits may be necessary before the extended scope can be formally approved.

TOP TIP

Be prepared to justify the scope of your BCMS to the auditor. They will want to understand how you have arrived at the scope and why you may have excluded any particular products and services.

ACTION SHEET

Taking into consideration what you have read about scoping a BCMS in this chapter, write down here the key considerations for your organisation's BCMS scope.

TOP MANAGEMENT RESPONSIBILITIES WITH RESPECT TO THE MANAGEMENT SYSTEM

The term 'top management' is frequently used in management systems and is aimed at a person, or group of people, who directs and controls an organisation at the highest level. Who is actually deemed to fit the criteria will depend on the size and complexity of the organisation and could vary from members of the corporate board to a sole proprietor of a small independent business. As mentioned before, it is your responsibility to apply the requirements of the standard in a way that suits your organisation, and so who you consider to be your top management (team) will vary. For a BCMS, it is advisable to nominate a senior manager to be accountable for its implementation and maintenance. This person is likely (but not obliged) to be part of top management. They may be called the Business Continuity Sponsor.

Commitment and Involvement

It cannot be over emphasised how important the role and involvement of top management is both during the implementation and maintenance phases of your BCMS. Ideally, the drive to implement such a system will have originated from top management and their commitment will be self evident, but this is not always the case. Where the initiative has grown from within the organisation (possibly someone has come from another business which successfully implemented a BCMS), there will be a need to convince top management that there are tangible benefits to undertaking such a programme. After all, why would top management, responsible for the ongoing profitability and success of the business, choose to commit resources to something that may never be used in earnest?

Top management will have different areas of focus and priorities depending on the nature and structure of the business. However, here are some of the main benefits of implementing a BCMS which you should highlight (in whatever style you think appropriate) to your top management:

- Competitive advantage;
- Supply chain rigour (and possibly a requirement);
- Better able to respond to the needs and expectations of interested parties;
- Financial benefits (possibly through insurance premiums) and through the ability to maintain predetermined business operation levels during times of disruption;
- Strengthened tendering process and outcome;
- Improved recruitment and retention rates by having better structured and controlled business processes;
- Consistent performance across sites, and staff who have a broader awareness of the business;
- Protection of brand and reputation through predetermined planning arrangements;
- A driver for continual improvement;
- If certification is being considered, this will also provide additional rigidity through external, independent audits as well as competitive advantage.

Responsibilities

In order for you to brief top management appropriately during the planning stage of your BCMS, and looking at ISO 22301 specifically, their obligations are clear.

Top management shall:

- Demonstrate leadership with respect to the BCMS;
- Demonstrate its commitment by[9]:

    o ensuring the BCMS is compatible with the strategic direction of the organisation;

    o integrating the BCMS requirements into the organisation's business processes;

    o ensuring the resources needed for the BCMS are available;

    o communicating the importance of effective business continuity management and conforming to the BCMS requirements;

    o ensuring that the BCMS achieves its intended outcomes;

    o directing and supporting continual improvement.

- Establish a BC policy;
- Ensure BCMS objectives and plans are established;
- Establish roles, responsibilities and competencies for BCM;
- Appoint one or more persons to be responsible for the BCMS with the appropriate authority and competencies to be accountable for the implementation and maintenance of the BCMS[10].

Top management shall ensure that the responsibilities and authorities for relevant roles are assigned and communicated within the organisation by:

- defining the criteria for accepting risks and the acceptable levels of risk;
- actively engaging in exercising and testing;
- ensuring that internal audits of the BCMS are conducted;
- conducting management reviews of the BCMS;
- demonstrating its commitment to continual improvement.

(Source: ISO 22301:2012)

---

[9] Reference to 'business' is to be interpreted broadly to mean those activities that are core to the purpose of the organisation's existence.

[10] These persons can hold other responsibilities within the organisation.

Obtaining top management commitment

To succeed in business it is necessary to make others see things as you see them.

Aristotle Onassis

Selling the benefits of a BCMS to top management can be challenging. You should get to know who you will be pitching your message to. What are their areas of interest in the business and what is most likely to get their attention? Are they financially driven, operationally minded or focused on the regulators? Knowing this will enable you to focus your proposal appropriately. You should also understand the dynamics of the top management team. Who is most likely to be receptive to the idea and who least in favour? Do not start by pitching to the person who is least likely to see the benefits of a BCMS. Also, decide whether it would be better to meet one member of top management on their own first, in order to test the water and get their support to proceed.

Preparing your pitch

Make sure that you have put together as strong a case as possible before asking for time in their busy schedules. Try and anticipate their questions and have the answers ready. By formulating your plan in this way, it will show management that you are serious about business continuity and the benefits of implementing a BCMS.

TOP TIP

Top management commitment and support must be ongoing and not just during the implementation phase of your BCMS. Make sure you engage them in exercises and other activities where the staff will see them getting involved!

MANAGEMENT SYSTEM DOCUMENTATION

Management systems often require a fair amount of documentation. However, it is pleasing to see that recognition is now given in standards to the progressive nature of the way information may be produced and stored. We can now move forward from the days when reams of paper based documents and manuals gathered dust on shelves in the office!

Standards clearly state their procedural requirements and which ones must be documented. Remember the definition of a procedure at the start of this chapter. It stated that not all procedures need to be documented, so check the wording carefully when implementing the standard.

In order to manage your documentation efficiently and effectively it needs to be controlled. This will require that you have a method of identifying your documents, for example by allocating reference numbers and issue dates. Establish a process for approving and reviewing documents, controlling their distribution to their intended audience and storing them safely in such a way that they are readily accessible for use. You should also determine how long you will retain each document for, based on legal requirements and internal protocols.

Many people still like to refer to paper based documentation and will print out endless pages of documents in order to satisfy this need. In order to prevent out-of-date documents being referred to long after their original publication, consider implementing a system whereby it is made clear that when a document is printed, it becomes uncontrolled and not to be relied upon as the latest version. This could be by way of a warning message on every page.

IMPROVEMENT

If you do not know how to ask the right question, you discover nothing.

W. Edwards Deming

One of the key outputs from operating a management system is to derive a method or methods for improving its effectiveness. As has already been said, users of management systems are no longer satisfied with simply complying with a set of requirements. They are now looking for added value and this often comes in the form of business improvements.

Nonconformity and corrective action
To help improve your BCMS you should include a review of its weaknesses. Whether your organisation chooses to use the term **nonconformity** or something less severe, recording these issues in a centrally controlled system will help the review process to identify the root cause, corrective action taken and the analysis of trends should they exist. It will also help ensure that the same or similar nonconformities do not arise elsewhere.

Continual Improvement
It can be daunting setting out to implement your first management system. You read about the need to 'continually improve' it, but you may not understand how and when to go about this. Because there are recognised controls in place as part of all management systems, these are where you should start to look for improvement opportunities.

Remember, if you improve your management system, you should ultimately improve your business operation.

TOP TIP

Here are some suggested BCMS activities which will support your improvement process:

- Implement a succession planning programme;
- The ongoing use and review of the BC policy;
- The review of BC objectives (to ensure that they are measurable and continue to reflect the needs of the business);
- The review of audit findings (these should be from internal and external audits);
- Maintain a programme of BCM awareness events throughout the organisation to ensure breadth of knowledge across all business levels;
- The review and analysis of events such as exercises, incidents and industry wide developments;
- The review of BCM arrangements including outputs from the business impact analysis and risk assessment processes;
- The identification and review of corrective actions (possibly accessed through a formal logging system);
- Review performance metrics used to ensure they continue to reflect the needs of the organisation;
- Implement best practices across multiple sites to encourage consistency of BCM approach;
- Conduct periodical reviews of the organisation's risk appetite in order to detect gradual shifts in risk acceptance levels;
- Consider critical supply chain links and identify opportunities to audit or review these with your suppliers in order to develop greater understanding and resiliency between parties.

Managing expectations

As with all other aspects of a management system, responsibility for the improvement of the system should be allocated to ensure ownership and accountability. All staff should be encouraged to participate in identifying improvements to what is essentially **their** management system. Over time, your aim should be to develop a culture of improvement and 'can do' attitude throughout the organisation.

Your management system will need time to establish itself before improvements can be identified. This is an area which should be considered as the system matures, by both internal and external auditors. It is part of their role to ensure that the organisation continues to strive for excellence! Of course, it goes without saying that none of this will be possible without the support and encouragement of the top management team.

ACTION SHEET

As your BCMS develops and you undertake more of the control requirements (audits, reviews, exercises etc.) make a note here of possible improvements to the system.

WRITING POLICIES AND SETTING OBJECTIVES

Actions to address risks and opportunities

As a pre cursor to developing your policy and objectives you should review the most important requirements of the business and what might prevent it from operating normally. Consider your customers and what they expect from you and then think about what might prevent the organisation from achieving this. Where you identify issues which you feel should be addressed, agree suitable actions, build these into your BCMS and remember to review whether the actions have been effective.

Management system policy

A fundamental element of the planning phase of the PDCA model is the development of a policy which lays out the foundations of the management system. The requirements of a policy are generic and are summarised below. The policy will:

- be appropriate to the organisations' activities and purpose;
- commit the management system to adhering to any requirements, be they legal or otherwise, that determine the organisation's ability to operate;
- provide a framework for establishing and reviewing objectives;
- include a commitment to the continual improvement of the BCMS;

- be implemented and be subject to periodical reviews;

- be made available to interested parties through pre determined forms of communication.

And that is before you have even written the policy!

Each of the above requirements is laid out in the standard and must be addressed. How you choose to write and present your policy is up to you and you should take into consideration how your organisation usually presents such information. However, you should bear in mind that a policy document such as this may appear dry to its intended audience and so should be kept brief.

You have already read that top management are responsible for the policy and, whilst they may not actually write the document itself, they should be encouraged to sign it. Their signature is a way of demonstrating to readers that they have endorsed the policy and take its purpose seriously. Ideally, the policy should then be made available at points where its intended audience will read it and take its message on board.

Policy reviews are generally conducted as part of the management review process. Whilst this forum is appropriate, on account of its constituents, it should be remembered that the aim of the review is to ensure that what was intended by the company at the time of writing is still relevant. For example, because of various factors, the organisation's attitude to risk may have altered, its activities changed or it may be affected by new legislation. The review process should demonstrate such consideration.

Setting appropriate objectives
As with writing a policy, setting objectives forms part of the planning phase of PDCA. These objectives should take into consideration aspects relating to the organisation's business, strategy and legal or other requirements relevant to the particular management system – in our case, the BCMS. They should also encourage continual improvement and wherever practicable, objectives should be measurable. Owners should be allocated to the objectives in order to maintain focus on their achievement.

To be credible, objectives must be reviewed periodically. An appropriate forum for this would be the management review. Where performance is not achieving a stated objective, a review programme should be implemented to consider what can be done to improve performance. As with establishing the policy, it falls to top management to ensure that objectives are being met.

Following the above advice, typical BCMS objectives may include:

(1) To effectively manage an incident that may impact the business, thus ensuring the requirements of all key stakeholders are met.

(2) To provide continuity of service to clients in the event of a business disruption by ensuring that key services are resumed within agreed timescales.

(3) To minimise the potential impact a business disruption would have on the company and its reputation (difficult to measure!).

(4) Customer expectations and service levels are managed to ensure customer retention.

TOP TIP

To maximise staff buy-in, keep your BC policy and objectives short and straightforward.

Retain your policy separately from other BCMS documentation. This will help maintain its focus.

ACTION SHEET

Use this space to write down some ideas for what you want your BCMS objectives to achieve.

ALLOCATION OF SUITABLE RESOURCES

As with any new piece of work, you will look at what resources you need and decide whether you should bring in additional support. Developing your BCMS is no different. In fact, this is an area of significant focus in management system standards so that proper consideration is given to ensuring the most suitable resources are deployed.

First of all you need to be clear about your resource requirements. Do not forget that this extends far beyond people, and also includes the allocation of time, space and equipment. Ultimately, this comes down to money and how much of an investment top management is prepared to make in a BCMS. (You will remember the pitch that you made to your top management? You should have included the resources that you need in this).

When identifying the resources needed, you should think about all the elements that go to make up developing and maintaining your BCMS. Consider the questions in Table 2.5 and how you might respond.

DETERMINING COMPETENCIES

Having identified resources required for the BCMS in general terms, you must consider what competency requirements each person requires in order for them carry out their BCMS duties effectively. This will shape how you decide to select named individuals. Competency may be achieved through education, training and/or experience and it is for you to determine what is appropriate for each person, based on their role in the BCMS.

A common oversight is when the BCMS activities are not sufficiently broken down to enable the best resource to be allocated. For example, instead of identifying a list of resource similar to that in Table 2.5, just a Business Continuity Manager is identified as BCMS resource. Worse still, no competencies are identified and an assumption made that the person will learn on the job.

Only by considering all the BCMS roles that you intend to deploy can you then determine appropriate competencies, how these might be obtained, evaluated and maintained.

One way of tracking BCMS competencies is to produce a matrix. This can then be monitored for who has achieved their competency levels, the effectiveness of this process and how their competency levels are to be maintained. An example is found in Table 2.6.

Keeping an eye on the future

It is too easy to rely on one person and allocate them sole responsibility for the BCMS. This is particularly true when they come with, or acquire, specialist BCM knowledge which is not available elsewhere in the organisation. We do not encourage our business to rely on a single client so why would we tolerate the risk of losing our sole BCMS resource?

Table 2.5 Identifying resources

Consideration	Your Response
1. Ownership of the management system itself and who will be directly involved with its development and maintenance. (This may be different people over time.)	
2. Who should act as Sponsor of the BCMS and owner of the BC Policy?	
3. Where will your BCMS be located and accessed through? Will it require additional IT infrastructure and support or will it be a paper based system?	
4. Do you have existing internal management system auditors who can be cross trained in BC, do you require additional internal resource or might you consider outsourcing this function to an independent expert?	
5. How do you intend to implement your business impact analysis? Will you include a broad range of staff or simply work with your management team? How much time have you set aside for this exercise?	
6. Do you have existing resource that reviews business risks? Would it be appropriate to extend their remit to fulfil BCMS requirements? Are there tools that you use for this and, if so, are they adequate for the BCMS requirements?	
7. Are you intending to manage the BCMS from a central point and coordinate activities from there or is your preference to devolve responsibility to local offices?	

(Continued)

Table 2.5 *(Continued)*

Consideration	Your Response
8. Do you currently have suitable personnel to act as spokes-people for the business? Have they been adequately trained and rehearsed their role? If not, how do you intend to address this?	
9. Does your organisation have trained resource to recognise when staff may be displaying stress related symptoms resulting from an incident? Would this normally fall to Human Resources to manage?	
10. Who would you expect to use for running your BC exercises? What skills would you look for in this role?	
11. Who would you expect to act as plan owners and participants in the event of invocation? Would additional training be required for them to undertake this role? Who would provide this and what would be included in the training?	
12. Do you have alternative sites that can be used to transfer staff and activities to in the event of an incident? How sustainable is this option? If not, would you consider third party recovery options? Consider any budgetary constraints.	
13. Who would be responsible for the analysis of BCMS information and the continual improvement of the BCMS?	

Table 2.6 Tracking BCMS competencies

BCMS role	BCMS awareness level required High/Medium/Low	BCMS knowledge required	Method of achieving competency level	Competency evaluation	Competency achieved? Yes/Part/No	Maintaining competency levels
BC Manager	H	Comprehensive knowledge of ISO 22301 and management systems in general	Attend professional training course(s) addressing ISO 22301, BCM requirements	Pass certificate for test of understanding where supplied by trainer		Attend standard update events
		BCM technical knowledge of BIA (business impact analysis), risk management, writing plans	Consider formal BCM qualification e.g. BCI certificate	Practical results of implementing BCM arrangements, through the results of exercises, invocations etc.		Network with other BC Managers
			Dependent on previous work experience.			Practical work experience
		People management skills	Training or on the job learning	Result of exercises and lessons learned		Successful results of external audits (where appropriate)
		Running exercises				

(Continued)

Table 2.6 *(Continued)*

BCMS role	BCMS awareness level required High/Medium/Low	BCMS knowledge required	Method of achieving competency level	Competency evaluation	Competency achieved? Yes/Part/No	Maintaining competency levels
Internal Auditor	M	Auditor qualification in BCMS standard or other management system with additional training for business continuity elements	Attend formal BCMS training course (or use existing management system qualification and attend transition course for BCMS)	Review of audit report to ascertain depth of knowledge, findings raised and general auditing skills		Undertake refresher standard training as appropriate
		Thorough knowledge of relevant BCMS standard, requirements and examples of evidence.	Undertake a number of internal BCMS audits under supervision (if appropriate)			Undertake periodical internal audits
		Ability to know when a BCMS system is effective				Results of external audits do not identify too many surprises

(Continued)

Table 2.6 (Continued)

BCMS role	BCMS awareness level required High/Medium/Low	BCMS knowledge required	Method of achieving competency level	Competency evaluation	Competency achieved? Yes/Part/No	Maintaining competency levels
BC Sponsor	M	General awareness and understanding of business continuity management and the BCMS. The aims and objectives and the need for top management support for the policy	Internal awareness training possibly provided by the BC Manager	Most likely to be demonstrated through their ongoing support and input to the BCMS		Periodical review of BC Policy and other BCMS documentation – possibly via Management Review meetings Involvement in BC exercises

(Continued)

Table 2.6 (*Continued*)

BCMS role	BCMS awareness level required High/Medium/ Low	BCMS knowledge required	Method of achieving competency level	Competency evaluation	Competency achieved? Yes/Part/No	Maintaining competency levels
BIA coordi-nator	M	General awareness of what a BCMS contains Detailed practical knowledge of how a BIA is developed and what is required. The abil-ity to assess the contents of a BIA and to know what is reasonable Good working knowledge of the business and its activities	Training from the BC Manager or from an external training provider Work experience	Review of BIA content BC Manager tests the accuracy of the information provided and how it links with the plans Test assumptions made through exercising the plans		Periodical review of BIA's (require-ment of a BCMS) Refresher BCMS training as appropriate

Experience has shown me that some individuals really take to BC and all that it stands for, whilst others simply view it as just another job they have to squeeze in to their day. Where someone shows an aptitude for running an exercise, getting more involved with audits or any other aspect of running the BCMS, they should be encouraged. They might even be the organisation's next Business Continuity Manager.

Succession planning should form part of every BCMS and your own BCM knowledge pool is a great place to start.

TOP TIP

Be prepared to justify to the auditor why someone has been allocated a specific role within your BCMS. You should be able to demonstrate what competencies are required for the role and how that person fulfils those requirements, either currently or through a clear development plan.

ACTION SHEET

Consider the BCMS roles you expect to create and, against each one, write down the competency requirements you consider appropriate.

EVALUATION OF THE PERFORMANCE AND EFFECTIVENESS OF THE MANAGEMENT SYSTEM

Having implemented the requirements of the standard, you will want to know that it is meeting its objectives and giving you what you require as an operational system. Surprisingly, this is an area often overlooked, with focus placed only on the 'Do' phase of the PDCA model. If you are seeking certification, this is an area that the auditor will expect to see being developed and, as your system matures, their expectation levels will increase too!

As an organisation, you will have decided what you want to measure. But how should you measure performance? Below are some recognised ways of evaluating how your management system is performing.

Internal audit

This is your opportunity to formally check whether your management system is operating in a way that complies with the requirements of the standard as well as your internal procedures.

As with other management system resources, the internal auditor must be competent to carry out the necessary duties. You will have determined what these competency levels are as part of your management system implementation. The auditor must be independent of the area they are auditing in order to be objective and impartial. This can cause difficulties in very small organisations and a pragmatic view should be taken in such instances.

Internal audits must be planned by way of an audit programme. This programme will include who will do what, when and how they will report their findings. Audits are to be scheduled and prioritised based on the results of previous audits and the importance of the activities. Audits should have an individual scope and the overall programme must cover the entire scope of the management system.

To maximise the value of your internal audits, the findings are to be reviewed and actions agreed which will improve the management system and operational processes of the business.

Management review

One of the responsibilities of top management is to periodically review the performance of the management system and to consider whether it is still meeting its objectives. How you conduct these meetings is up to you and some senior managers have a preferred way of reviewing information presented to them. What is important is that they take the opportunity to consider both the detail and the overall effectiveness of the system. The standard helpfully gives you an indication of what should be included in these meetings (known as 'inputs') and this should be used as the basis for the agenda, adding any local issues as appropriate.

Management review meetings need to be minuted and actions allocated to specific people. Unless this is done, you will find it difficult to demonstrate that you have followed up actions and that you have reviewed whether they were effective. Someone needs to take ownership of this process and ensure that changes are made to the management system as a result of these meetings (known as 'outputs').

Nonconformity and corrective action review

Nonconformities and corrective actions should be reviewed collectively and objectively to determine whether trends exist which might uncover an underlying weakness in the BCMS. Findings should be fed into the management review process in order to keep top management informed, and also the findings acted upon as soon as possible to prevent occasional instances developing into potentially regular occurrences.

Other metrics to help evaluate the performance of your BCMS might include near misses and false alarms, responses to actual incidents and results of exercises and call tree test responses. For more information about selecting the most appropriate metrics for your organisation and how to evaluate the performance of your BCMS, go to **Appendix A**.

TOP TIP

The requirement to 'monitor performance' and 'analyse' the effectiveness of your management system is significant and for good reason. Do not let yourself get too focused on the 'Do' of the PDCA cycle to the detriment of the 'Check' and 'Act' phases.

ACTION SHEET

Make a note here of what you consider are the over arching objectives of your BCMS and what you expect to see as evidence that it is working effectively.

ALIGNMENT WITH OR CERTIFICATION TO ISO 22301? WHICH PATH SHOULD I CHOOSE?

Many organisations start out on their BCMS journey intending to align themselves with the standard but not seeking third party certification. In this final section on management systems we look at why this might be, whether the next step to certification really is that big and the advantages and disadvantages of both options.

Alignment

Operating 'in line with' a business continuity standard infers the adoption of the BCMS principles. But what does this mean to a business or its customers? Does it only cover part of the business or all of its key products or services? There is no mechanism for confirming this.

The drivers for implementing a BCMS differ between organisations. Some may begin within the business whilst others look externally at stakeholder requirements. Both are equally valid and may depend on the nature of the business or its customer base. These drivers may also determine whether the business chooses to be aligned to the standard or whether they are seeking certification.

The difficulty comes when the word 'alignment' is used without justification. It is an easy claim to make, but can potentially devalue the hard work of those organisations which have implemented a full BCMS.

There are a number of advantages to being aligned to a standard

- You have the benchmark of a respected standard by which to measure your BCMS.

- It provides a framework for a robust BCMS.

- There are no costs of certification.

- Insurers, suppliers and other stakeholders may look favourably on your BC arrangements.

- You may gain competitive advantage.

- You have no external audit requirement.

- It will be easier to go through the certification process if and when you are ready.

The disadvantages of being aligned to a standard

- You have no formal approval mark by a recognised third party.

- There is a risk that a lack of external controls may stop you maintaining the BCMS.

- You might lose potential clients to certified organisations.

- Often, greater board level 'management' is required to maintain the BCMS principles.

Certification to ISO 22301

There's a misunderstanding that moving from alignment to certification is a major exercise. This does not have to be the case.

If you are already truly aligned to the standard, then there is no reason why going for certification should be a burden. It is only if you are not fully aligned that you will have to work hard to satisfy the external audit process.

TOP TIP

Issues to consider prior to certification in which you need confidence and might not otherwise regard as important:

- Is your BCMS embedded into your organisation?

    o How do you demonstrate this?

- Have you addressed all the requirements of a BCMS?

- How is this information made available to staff?

- Are you confident that your staff, if asked, could explain their role during an incident?

- Do you have documentary evidence of the outcomes of your audits, review meetings and exercises?

Winning more business with a business continuity management system

Many organisations require certification to a BCMS standard for tendering or supply chain purposes. As BC standards grow in recognition, this trend is likely to continue. You should consider whether your business can afford **not** to be certified, particularly if you are competing with organisations which are. There is also pride felt by the staff in organisations which have achieved certification. The certificate is often displayed in public areas and staff feel part of that success.

The advantages of being certified to ISO 22301

- You will have a consistent approach to BCM across the organisation.

- Your BCMS is verified by a recognised certification body.

- You will have a competitive edge.

- You can use it in marketing initiatives through the display of your certificate and/or logo.

- There is no quibble evidence available to submit for tenders and supplier questionnaires.

- A BCMS is a driver for continual improvement across the organisation.

The disadvantages of certification to ISO 22301

Initial and annual cost to achieve and maintain certification can be seen as a disadvantage. The cost can vary greatly depending on the scope of your BCMS, but should not be the sole reason for not pursuing certification.

CONCLUSION: SHOULD MY ORGANISATION CONSIDER CERTIFICATION?

Achieving certification to an internationally recognised standard moves your organisation up to the best in class in your industry. Whether the decision is made within the business or is driven by external factors, it will encourage a level of discipline which is unlikely to be there otherwise. Also, your clients, current and future, might start asking for objective evidence of your BCM arrangements and how they are maintained. Certification offers this.

For more information and practical advice about what to expect if your organisation intends to seek certification, go to Chapter 4: The Certification Process.

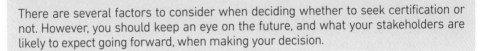

TOP TIP

There are several factors to consider when deciding whether to seek certification or not. However, you should keep an eye on the future, and what your stakeholders are likely to expect going forward, when making your decision.

ACTION SHEET

Has your organisation made its decision about whether to seek alignment or certification to ISO 22301?

Either way, based on the information provided in this chapter (and any other relevant factors), list what considerations you believe your organisation should take into account when reaching its decision.

SUMMARY

(1) The technical and system requirements of your BCMS are **equally** important to its success.

(2) Develop a BCMS that reflects the needs and culture of **your** organisation.

(3) Consider your BCMS scope carefully. Remember that you can extend it at a later date.

(4) If you opt to exclude particular products or services, make sure you can justify this decision both internally and externally.

(5) Be clear on your reasons for implementing a BCMS and what benefits you wish to gain from it.

(6) In order to make the BCMS accessible to staff, utilise existing systems and communication methods, such as the intranet or company magazine.

(7) Ensure sufficient independence when reviewing BCMS performance to gain maximum benefit.

(8) Make sure you have appropriate and competent resource in place to operate your BCMS and top management appreciate the importance of this for its success.

(9) Select your internal audit resource carefully to meet competency requirements and independence from the day to day operation of the BCMS.

(10) Management reviews are the organisation's opportunity to consider the operational effectiveness of the BCMS and how this sits with strategic business requirements so make sure the right people attend.

3 BUSINESS CONTINUITY FROM A MANAGEMENT SYSTEM PERSPECTIVE

PURPOSE AND OBJECTIVE

In this chapter we focus on the practical elements of business continuity management and consider them from a management system perspective: Where should the emphasis be when it comes to fitting your BCM arrangements into a management system?

We will use the six phases of the BCM lifecycle as our focal point and offer Top Tips for you to consider when developing your BCMS. Unlike BS 25999, ISO 22301 does not make reference to the lifecycle directly but provides an explanation of the PDCA model through its reference to the lifecycle's constituent parts (Source: ISO 22301:2012 The Plan Do Check Act Model, Table 1). The lifecycle's elements clearly communicate the professional practices of BCM and therefore remain a useful tool. In order for you to become familiar with ISO 22301 terminologies this section includes reference to both.

After reading this section you should be able to maximise the benefits of your BCMS whilst ensuring you have a robust BCM programme in place.

Further, detailed, information can be found in The BCI Good Practice Guidelines 2010.

THE BCM LIFECYCLE

The BCM lifecycle which we recognise today was published in BS 25999 Part 1, in 2006. It clearly depicts the six phased approach to developing and maintaining a BC programme and can be applied to any organisation, irrespective of its size and industry sector (see Figure 3.1).

Figure 3.1 The BCM Lifecycle

Source: BS 25999-1:2006

We will consider the phases in the following sequence:

(1) BCM programme management

(2) Understand the organisation

(3) Determining BCM strategy

(4) Developing and implementing a BCM response

(5) Exercising, maintaining and reviewing

(6) Embedding BCM in the organisation's culture.

POSITIONING THE BCM LIFECYCLE WITH YOUR BCMS

Table 3.1 identifies the core elements of business continuity management and considers how each one should be treated in order to meet the requirements of a BCMS.

Table 3.1 Elements of business continuity management

Elements of BCM programme management	BCMS Top Tips 
The BCM programme will be aligned to the organisation's overarching strategy, business plan and objectives.	When considering business continuity objectives, be sure to demonstrate that there is a link between these and the organisation's strategic objectives and responsibility for achieving them is allocated and clearly understood.
Position the programme so it is in step with the organisation's culture and style of management.	How the organisation chooses to approach its BCM programme and the requirements of the standard should be comparable with the complexity of the business and the environment in which it operates. This is particularly the case for smaller businesses not having the capacity or need for a complex programme.
	To be accepted within the organisation, your BCMS should be developed as if it was part of the current fabric of the business. Staff are more likely to buy into the new system if there are elements of familiarity to it.
Understand the benefits of the programme to both internal and external stakeholders and identify ways to maximise these benefits.	Having a clear view of how you wish to include key stakeholders/interested parties within your BCM programme will help you develop a more robust system from the outset.
Determine the scope of the BCM programme, usually in terms of products and services, and consider the impact of outsourced activities and whether to include them. Consideration is also required about the role played by legislation, regulation or contractual responsibilities in the proposed BCM programme.	Where the organisation makes a deliberate choice to limit its scope with a view to extending it later, the organisation will benefit if it is able to plan the scope's expansion in terms of time and resource. Such a plan will help support the case for a restricted scope to internal and external stakeholders.

(Continued)

Table 3.1 (Continued)

Elements of BCM programme management	BCMS Top Tips
Identify the BCM resource needed and how it will work with top management to ensure its direct involvement.	The need to engage top management at the earliest stage (preferably before implementation has started) and to stress the importance of its visible leadership of the programme cannot be over emphasised.
	BCMS roles, responsibilities and authorities must be considered and communicated to the incumbent and their line manager. The clear allocation of authorities, where these differ from routine work is critical in order for quick decisions to be made during an incident.
	A clear method of establishing competency requirements for each BCMS role is important and a route to achieving these (with documentary evidence to support this) is required.
Development and communication of a BCM Policy encompassing the key elements of the programme, its objectives and ownership by top management.	The organisation should carefully consider how it communicates its BCM policy so that it is accessible to all interested parties and, more importantly, its intent understood.
A clear implementation programme, and a method for managing and developing its sustainability in line with business needs, is required.	Periodical reviews of the BCM programme will ensure that it remains in line with the business needs. Top management should take responsibility for this.
An ongoing programme review process and flexible attitude towards organisational change is required.	Methods of reviewing the performance and effectiveness of the BCMS including BCM capabilities are principally through management review, internal audit and self assessment. Metrics to determine performance levels should be aligned to the needs of the organisation and results of the analysis recorded, considered and acted upon as necessary.
BCM documentation must be appropriate for the organisation, clear, accessible and manageable.	Documentation must be controlled to ensure it remains up to date and accessible. Responsibility for this should be allocated at the development stage so that there is visible ownership within the BCMS.

BCM programme management

Programme management is at the core of BCM. It is not only critical to the development of a BCM capability but also to the ongoing success of it. In short, it gives BCM purpose and direction.

ACTION SHEET

Make a note of any actions that you have thought of whilst reading about BCM programme management.

Understand the organisation

In order to develop an effective BCM programme, the organisation has to fully understand its business objectives and strategic aims as well as its obligations towards its stakeholders. It must also be clear how a disruption to business activities might impact on its ability to continue trading. An appreciation of the **context** of the organisation is also required.

To understand your organisation thoroughly, you need to undertake a BIA, review resource requirements and conduct a risk assessment of your most important and time-critical business activities (see Table 3.2).

Table 3.2 Elements of 'understand the organisation'

Elements of 'understand the organisation'	💡 BCMS Top Tips
Seek top management support to conduct a BIA.	The BIA is the backbone of a meaningful BCM programme. Do not underestimate the time and resource required to get the most out of this process and make sure you get top management buy-in before you start! This includes a clear understanding of who will be involved.
Determine the most appropriate method of conducting a BIA for your organisation and identify the resources to do it.	If you are carrying out a BIA for the first time, keep it simple. Let it evolve and mature over time.
Agree whether the BIA will be undertaken after the scope of the BCM programme has been agreed or whether it will be used to determine the scope after completion of the exercise.	It may help to have an outline scope defined before conducting the BIA. This will help with the allocation of resources. If the results of the BIA show up activities not initially considered a priority, these may be added to the final scope.
Identifying the impacts of a disruption at various levels of an organisation will identify different issues and influence how priorities are set.	By establishing a systematic approach to defining the BIA's criteria for measuring the impacts a disruption may have on the organisation, this can be applied across different levels of the organisation.
Consider how activities are impacted over time and how this varies for different activities, products and services.	Think carefully how you plan to bracket timeframes within the BIA. Make sure that they reflect the nature of the business and the needs and expectations of interested parties. (It is too easy to default to timescales applied by others without understanding their pertinence.)

(Continued)

Table 3.2 *(Continued)*

Elements of 'understand the organisation'	BCMS Top Tips 
Agree a method for determining what activities are most time critical to the organisation and agree the basis for their prioritisation.	Remember that what you consider to be a less important activity today may become a priority tomorrow and should still form part of your BIA review process. Do not automatically disregard activities which you have not classified as 'top priority'.
Identify the dependencies relied upon to carry out business activities. These may be internal and external to the organisation.	Try a brainstorming exercise to identify all the organisation's dependencies. By broadening the reach of this thought process, you will be surprised what gets uncovered!
Identify the resources (people, premises, technology, information, supplies, equipment, stakeholders) required to support the activities upon resumption.	Remember to consider how quickly backlogs can occur. This will depend on the nature of the activity but will need to be built in to resource planning during invocation and beyond.
Determine the maximum time after which the organisation's viability is irreparably damaged if product or service delivery cannot continue. This will include estimating how long you believe your customers will be prepared to tolerate disruption to their service delivery from you.	Timescales are likely to vary for different products and services and this variation will help the organisation prioritise its recovery activities. These are not cast in stone and real life incidents and the results of exercises will provide valuable insight into their validity. Remember that you do not have to wait until a scheduled review of the BIA to make changes to it.
Establish a review process once the BIA has been completed and obtain top management sign off before proceeding.	Try and maintain a level of independence with this review. Consider the needs of the organisation and its overall strategy and do not be swayed by individuals who try and tell you that what they do is the most important thing in the business.

(Continued)

Table 3.2 (*Continued*)

Elements of 'understand the organisation'	BCMS Top Tips
Based on the results of the BIA, carry out a risk assessment of the prioritised activities. As well as identifying particular threats, consider possible vulnerable resources.	Remember to focus your threat analysis on hazards that are relevant and appropriate. Include 'localised' threats to specific sites to demonstrate that proper consideration has been applied to this process.
Determine a suitable risk management model for your organisation taking into consideration any existing methods used. Risk criteria and scoring systems should be appropriate for the organisation and in line with its risk appetite.	Do not over complicate your risk management model, especially if your organisation is not used to proactive risks reviews. The model can be developed over time. Be clear with your criteria and scoring system and make sure that everyone involved in the risk management process applies the same model.
Identify risks considered to be unacceptable to the organisation (based on the predefined scoring system), review them, agree action to mitigate the risk and/or reduce the impact if realised.	When assessing and prioritising control measures, take into account the cost of such actions and the possible consequence of inaction in order to support the decision making process.
Establish a periodical risk review process.	Where possible, the organisation's aim should be to reduce, manage or eliminate significant risks. Risks which continue to be 'accepted' for prolonged periods should be questioned to make sure that complacency does not set in.

ACTION SHEET

Make a note of any actions that you have thought of whilst reading about how to under-stand the organisation.

Determining BCM strategy

Following the completion of the 'understand the organisation' phase, the business is in a position to consider options available to it which will enable the restoration of prioritised operations affected by a disruption. Options should be considered on strategic and tactical levels (see Table 3.3).

Table 3.3 Elements of determining BCM strategy

Elements of determining BCM strategy	BCMS Top Tips 
BCM strategies should be identified at both commercial and operational levels.	Be ready to demonstrate how you have selected your BCM strategies at both commercial and operational levels. What business considerations were taken into account, cost versus benefit and how top management commitment was obtained.
Examples of commercial strategies include the consideration of multiple site operation, alternative operation sites either owned or contracted for by the organisation and to subcontract or outsource some operations.	
Examples of operational (tactical) strategies include third party recovery site contract, home working, duplication of supplies, backup power facilities, multiple suppliers and information and data backup.	
Commercial strategies focus on the products and services within the BCM scope whereas operational strategies focus on the time-critical/prioritised activities supporting those products and services.	
BCM strategies are to be aligned to the organisation's risk appetite.	
BCM strategies are to be aligned to the organisation's strategic goals as well as closely linked to the results of the BIA and risk assessment.	Make sure BCM strategies reflect how the organisation has prioritised its activities. For example, if you are a law firm, you will need to focus on your people and their ability to access client and legal information quickly. Your strategies are likely to focus on areas such as IT and telecoms and document storage over finance and corporate hospitality.

(Continued)

Table 3.3 *(Continued)*

Elements of determining BCM strategy	BCMS Top Tips
BCM strategies must be in line with recovery timescales identified within the BIA.	Often BCM strategies will be chosen based on recovery time objectives identified as part of the BIA process so these must be realistic and well considered. Remember, the shorter the recovery time the more expensive the operational strategy is likely to be.
Be clear who the interested parties are when selecting BCM strategies.	You should consider the needs of interested parties and their expectations of your ability to continue business operations during and immediately after an incident. You may need to prioritise the activities in order to meet these expectations.
BCM strategies that require the allocation of resource must not conflict with each other.	You should apply stress tests to the strategies you have selected to make sure that if more than one is applied during an incident, the resources needed for one will not prevent another strategy being deployed.
BCM strategies must have the full support of top management. When making recommendations to top management, include cost projections and the effect of inaction.	Be realistic with your cost projections and prepare a business case where a BCM strategy may involve significant financial commitment. For example, your organisation might consider the need to contract with a recovery site provider and the cost should be weighed up against the cost to the business if it was unable to recover its operations quickly (in another way).
BCM strategies should be reviewed at least every 12 months to ensure they continue to reflect current organisational requirements.	Be mindful of changes within the organisation. For example, if it acquires additional business or sites, the need for contracting to alternative managed facilities may diminish.

ACTION SHEET

Make a note of any actions that you have thought of whilst reading about BCM strategies.

Developing and implementing a BCM response

Having taken time to fully understand the organisation and develop BCM strategies, the organisation is now in a position to develop business continuity **procedures** including its plan or plans. These plans will identify the resources and actions required to manage a disruption and resume prioritised activities (see Table 3.4).

Table 3.4 Elements of developing and implementing a BCM response

Elements of developing and implementing a BCM response	BCMS Top Tips
There are a number of stages for responding to an incident: • Emergency response • Incident management • BC • Recovery • Resumption. The extent of the plan(s) should reflect the makeup and complexity of the organisation and scope of BCM arrangements.	Plans must address the key stages of responding to an incident. However, the size and complexity of the organisation will determine how the plans are structured and integrated. There is no set way of structuring plans but they should sufficiently address the organisations' response needs. Plans should be accessible and understood by those with BCM responsibilities. Writing plans that are complex or difficult to follow will result in them being largely ignored in the event of invocation.
BC plans (this term may be used to refer to various plans aimed at different levels within the organisation) will cover strategic business areas such as external communications and stakeholder management, and prioritised operational activities such as payroll, project management or the provision of certain IT applications. There may also be specific plans covering individual threats, such as pandemic.	Generally, BC plans should be developed to minimise the **impact** of a threatening situation to the organisation rather than around broad scenarios such as fire, flood or earthquake. (Pandemic is a reasonable exception to this.)

(Continued)

Table 3.4 *(Continued)*

Elements of developing and implementing a BCM response	BCMS Top Tips
BC Plans should address three tiers of business activity:	How the organisation chooses to incorporate the three tiers will be determined by the size and complexity of the business (see first tip).
Strategic: Top management take direct responsibility for issues such as managing the media, business reputation, welfare of individuals and environmental/wider impacts from an incident.	The organisation can name their tiered plans as they wish to suit their culture.
Tactical: Management will oversee operations during an incident including the overall allocation of resource and coordination of activities.	
Operational: Business unit level focus on continuing predetermined prioritised activities which support the delivery of key products and services.	
BC plans can be produced in a number of ways and involve different people. The basis of developing plans should be to include:	It is important to develop a BC plan template that suits your organisation's needs. Try not to 'cut and paste' templates used by others unless the style and format reflects your own requirements.
• Information gathered from the BIA and Risk Assessment processes	Much of the information in Tactical and Operational BC plans may be generic to the organisation. However, it should be clear to users which areas relate specifically to their activities. It should not be lost amongst several pages of 'other' information.
• Lessons learned from previous incidents	
• Local information	
• The views of different staff/managers.	Make sure that BC plans remain flexible so that they can easily be adapted to different incident situations.

(Continued)

50

Table 3.4 *(Continued)*

Elements of developing and implementing a BCM response	BCMS Top Tips
The key aspects that form the basis of a BC plan are: • Purpose, scope and objectives • Roles and responsibilities • Invocation and stand down authority • Communications • Meeting points • Contact details • Key information to support the recovery of prioritised activities • Set of assumptions and known interdependencies.	Where possible, have more than one tested method of communicating with staff and other stakeholders during an incident. For example email and mobile phone or pager. Identify more than one meeting point. One on site and one away from the office. Information which is subject to change may be held in appendices. This will reduce the need to reproduce complete plans when, for example, contact details change and need updating.

(Continued)

51

Table 3.4 *(Continued)*

Elements of developing and implementing a BCM response	BCMS Top Tips
Action sheets and logs should form part of the plan (possibly as appendices). They should also be included along with other key information, in battle boxes and/or grab bags.	Make sure that any battle boxes/grab bags are placed in accessible and secure locations. For example at a security gate/office and secondary/third party recovery location.
	Include an inventory in the box/bag and ensure that whether locked or not, the contents are periodically checked, equipment remains operational (for example batteries remain charged) and that a record is kept of these inspections (a favourite for auditors).
All plans must include the roles, responsibilities and authorities of the response team.	The allocation of duties for managing BC plans should be carefully considered before appointment. Like all BCM roles, the individual must have the necessary competence for the role (which you will have predetermined), availability and the respect of his peers and managers.
	For example, it does not automatically have to be the job of the department manager.

ACTION SHEET

Make a note of any actions that you have thought of whilst reading about developing and implementing a BCM response.

Exercising, maintaining and reviewing BCM

Having developed and implemented a BCM response, you must now rehearse the arrangements to ensure those impacted by them become familiar with what happens upon invocation and beyond. You should also have a maintenance programme in place to make sure that your arrangements remain up to date and reflect current business needs (see Table 3.5).

Table 3.5 Elements of exercising, maintaining and reviewing BCM

Elements of exercising, maintaining and reviewing BCM	BCMS Top Tips
An exercise and test programme should be developed which covers all BC plans, information held within the plans and people who may be impacted by invocation.	Remember to involve interested parties in the exercise programme.
There are a number of recognised methods of exercising and testing BCM arrangements and the programme should reflect this. These include:	To ensure that you 'bring staff with you' on the BCM journey, the initial exercises should be simple. You can then build on them as confidence grows and there is greater familiarity with BCM arrangements.
• Call tree test	An established exercise programme should continue to include a broad range of exercises.
• IT tests	
• Desk top review	Exercise scenarios should be pertinent to the organisation, its strategy (including risk appetite) and take into consideration any local requirements, such as logistical issues.
• Walk through	
• Simulation/scenario	
• Partial exercise of prioritised activities	
• Full exercise including incident management response.	
When developing an exercise and test schedule, consider:	Exercises and tests should be progressive. Make sure weaknesses are retested until removed. Take into account new risks facing the organisation as a result of internal and external changes. Be sure to demonstrate continual improvement through your exercise programme.
• The results of previous exercises	
• Known threats	
• Stakeholder requirements	
• Cost	
• Variety in order to retain interest and focus.	

(Continued)

Table 3.5 *(Continued)*

Elements of exercising, maintaining and reviewing BCM	BCMS Top Tips 
The programme should be for a set timeframe, for example 12 months hence. It should be discussed with, and approved by, top management and be in line with budgetary requirements.	Exercises should take place on an ongoing basis. This will help staff become familiar with what is expected of them and provide assurance that incidents do not have to be too disruptive to their work life. By varying the type and involvement of staff, this should not impact the entire organisation too much.
Top management should take a proactive role in exercises.	Direct involvement in exercises by top management not only ensures they remain familiar with their responsibilities during an incident, but also demonstrates their support for BCM to staff.
Ensure that exercises to not expose the organisation to undue risk.	Consider the scheduling of exercises so that they do not occur during busy times for the business. Also consider what resource will be required for each exercise or test so that excessive burdens are not placed on remaining staff.
Each exercise and test should have a predetermined objective.	Remember to revisit the objective when carrying out the exercise review in order to conclude whether it has been met (or not). Make sure you document this in your report.
Individuals running and observing exercises and tests must be competent to do so.	As with other BCM competencies, these need to be predetermined. Consider the soft skills that are suited to this role, for example operating under stressful circumstances and applying attention to detail.
	Organisations may choose to involve external providers during some of the more complex exercises. This is fine, but ideally the skills required should be developed by those within the organisation to support ownership of the BCM programme.

(Continued)

Table 3.5 *(Continued)*

Elements of exercising, maintaining and reviewing BCM	BCMS Top Tips
All exercises and tests are to be formally reported and reviewed.	To support the continual improvement of the BCMS, the outcomes of the exercise or test are to be recorded along with lessons learned, improvement areas and follow up actions. Confirmation of whether the original objectives were achieved is also required.
	It should be evident that top management has sight of these reports and the opportunity to provide input to them. It may also be worthwhile sharing the results of exercises and tests with staff as a way of maintaining their BCMS awareness.
A BCM maintenance programme is required in order for all aspects of BCM to be reviewed and updated. A minimum review period should be set (ideally at least annually) and be flexible so that changes impacting the organisation are also considered and incorporated where necessary.	Encourage a culture which proactively develops your BCMS arrangements. This will ensure that there are not prolonged periods where changes affecting the organisation are not incorporated into the BCMS programme.
	Manage organisational expectations that the BIA, risk assessment, strategy and BC plans will all evolve and develop over time.
There should be clear ownership of the BCM maintenance and review programme.	The review of BC plans should be through named plan owners. They will have knowledge of localised changes and will be best placed to keep users informed of amendments.

ACTION SHEET

Make a note of any actions that you have thought of whilst reading about exercising, maintaining and reviewing BCM.

Embedding BCM in the organisation's culture

To be fully effective, the BCM programme must be embedded in the organisations' culture. That means that BCM becomes part of the organisation's core values. Understanding what the business expects in this respect, how it will achieve it and measuring its effectiveness all form part of the embedding process. Its approach to communication and BCM awareness must be flexible and maintained throughout the BCM Programmes' existence (see Table 3.6).

Table 3.6 Elements of embedding BCM in the organisation's culture

Elements of embedding BCM in the organisation's culture	BCMS Top Tips 
To develop a sustainable BCM culture within your organisation, you must first have a clear idea of the current awareness levels of BCM within the business. The results of analysis should then be compared to the level of awareness the organisation wishes to achieve, after which a programme can be developed.	This information will in part become clear when you conduct your BIA and Risk Assessment. Expectations should be managed carefully in order to avoid false hope or disappointment.
An organisations' culture develops over time and is heavily influenced by top management behaviour and attitude. To embed BCM into the organisation's culture effectively, top management must visibly support the programme as must the remaining management team and staff.	Top management is expected to maintain its support during and after the initial stages of BCM programme implementation. The effort required to achieve this should not be underestimated.
Where necessary, existing behaviour may be changed through knowledge and enlightenment. A BCM awareness programme should consider: ● Who will be responsible for implementing the programme ● What the programme will consist of ● When and how often specific awareness activities are to be deployed ● How the effectiveness of the programme is monitored ● The cost of running the programme (programme requires top management prior approval) ● Where the awareness, education and training will be obtained from ● What the acceptable minimum levels of achievement will be and by when.	What you decide to incorporate into your awareness programme will subconsciously be determined by the organisation's existing culture. You should choose methods that you believe your staff and interested parties will 'buy into'. What methods your organisation chooses is immaterial (within reason!) as long as you can measure greater awareness over time, improved performance during exercises and recovery from incidents.

Examples of methods of embedding BCM in the organisation's culture include:

- General staff briefings across the organisation
- Office poster campaigns
- Conducting a BIA
- Conducting risk assessments and maintaining a risk register
- Communicating risk acceptance levels amongst managers
- Writing BC plans
- Participation (at whatever level) in exercises and tests
- Participation in Business Continuity Awareness Week activities (in house or external)
- Specific BCM training, e.g. organising exercises, developing a BIA, auditing the BCMS
- BCM education courses
- Awareness and understanding of the BC policy and objectives
- Understanding the implications of not having BCM arrangements in place
- Ensuring individuals understand the impact a disruption might have on their role
- Communicating the results of exercises and feedback from a disruption.

ACTION SHEET

Make a note of any actions that you have thought of whilst reading about embedding BCM in the organisation's culture.

SUMMARY

(1) The BCM lifecycle should be viewed as an ongoing process rather than a one off exercise. Whilst not directly referred to in ISO 22301, it remains a useful tool for BCM resource.

(2) Develop the BCMS in line with the business's core strategy, aims and objectives.

(3) Establish a practical BCM programme which is straightforward and clear to everyone involved.

(4) In order to have effective BCM arrangements you need to understand the organisation, its key products and services, time-critical and prioritised activities and the needs and expectations of interested parties.

(5) BC strategies should reflect the needs and capabilities of the organisation and be aligned to its risk acceptance levels.

(6) Design your BCM response to sit comfortably with other operational requirements. Do not overcomplicate it.

(7) Be clear when allocating roles, responsibilities and authorities and rehearse these.

(8) A good way to develop closer partnerships with key suppliers is to include them in your exercise programme.

(9) Start your exercise programme with straight forward tests and develop their complexity over time.

(10) The post exercise review is equally important as the exercise itself.

(11) Embedding BCM into the organisation's culture is an ongoing process and one which should involve everyone working under the organisations' direction.

4 COMPARING ISO 22301 WITH BS 25999 AND UNDERSTANDING THE DIFFERENCES

PURPOSE AND OBJECTIVE

In this chapter we will compare and contrast ISO 22301 with BS 25999, paying particular attention to the format, approach and requirements of the ISO standard. The objective is to equip you with the information necessary for you to make an informed decision about how best to apply the requirements of the International Standard to your BCMS.

For organisations which have, or are working towards, certification to BS 25999, we will discuss what additional work may be needed to become compliant with ISO 22301 as well as what is involved with certificate transition.

HOW BCMS STANDARDS ARE PRODUCED

British Standards, such as BS 25999, are produced by BSI through authorised technical committees. These committees are made up, in part, of practitioners who work in the respective community, in this case BC, and whose technical, practical and academic experience is drawn upon to create a best practice management system standard. A British Standard may be applied worldwide. In addition, there are supporting published documents that build upon certain areas of BCM. Examples of these are PD 25111:2010 *BCM Guidance on human aspects of business continuity*, PD 25666:2010 *BCM Guidance on Exercising and Testing for Continuity and Contingency Programmes* and PD 25222:2011 *BCM Guidance on Supply Chain Continuity*. As the titles suggest, these documents are for guidance purposes only and so do not form part of specification standard requirements.

The International Organisation for Standardisation (ISO) is a worldwide federation of national bodies. As with British Standards, international standards are produced through technical committees and ISO member bodies are entitled to be represented on a technical committee. To put this into context, the ISO technical committee for ISO 22301 is made up of member bodies representing over 30 countries.

Whilst there are a number of differences between British and international standards, one of the most significant distinctions is the formal voting process which exists for draft international standards. Member bodies will exercise their right to vote on the proposed standard which, if to be published, requires at least 75 per cent approval by those casting a vote. As a result of this consensus approach, there are occasions when international standards may appear more generic when compared to national standards. This practice is not carried out as part of approving a British Standard.

As has already been discussed in Chapter 2, the production method of ISO Management System Standards is under review. ISO 22301 incorporates the proposed format of high level structure and terminology and it is anticipated that all subsequent International Management System Standards will follow this approach, including future revisions of existing ISO Management System Standards.

As is the case with other ISO management system standards, a 'series' of standards will be available for BCMSs.

- ISO 22301 *Societal security – Business Continuity Management Systems – Requirements*. This document is aimed at internal and external parties, including certification bodies, to assess an organisation's ability to meet its own business continuity needs and obligations.

- ISO 22313 *Societal security - Business Continuity Management Systems – Guidance*. Unlike BS 25999 Part 1, this document includes guidance on both BCM and BCMS.

- ISO 22300 *Societal security – Vocabulary*.

THE SIMILARITIES BETWEEN ISO 22301 AND BS 25999

Significantly, the ISO standard adopts the same management system approach as BS 25999. This means that the PDCA model remains the backbone of the standard as well as the common management system elements, discussed in Chapter 2. However, emphasis is now placed on each clause of ISO 22301 and which element of the PDCA model it represents. Of the seven implementation clauses, the first four represent the **Plan** requirements, providing us with a clear message as to where the main emphasis of ISO 22301 resides.

BS 25999, along with other respected national BC standards, has been key to the development of ISO 22301. We therefore see a number of familiar requirements:

- Business continuity policy and programme management
- BCM awareness and communication (embedding)
- Understanding the organisation through the BIA and risk assessment processes
- BC strategies
- BCM procedures
- Exercising and testing
- BCM performance review.

Whilst we are familiar with these components of BCM, it is important to note that some have different requirements in the ISO standard. We will now look at these and other aspects of the BCMS in more detail and consider the changes that have been introduced.

THE DIFFERENCES BETWEEN ISO 22301 AND BS 25999

ISO has built upon the British Standard and created a robust standard which is aimed at a global audience.

The differences between the standards reveal three key points:

(1) Terminology is aimed at an international audience; reference to ISO 22300, *Societal security – Terminology*, should provide greater clarity.

(2) ISO's aim to develop a generic structure for management system standards has placed additional focus on the need for planning, top management leadership, communication and BCMS performance evaluation.

(3) Business continuity practitioners expect a BCMS standard to address a broader range of issues and conditions potentially arising from a disruption. An example of this is the need to consider how stakeholder (otherwise known as interested party) relationships and supply chains may be impacted by a disruptive incident.

We will now consider these aspects in more detail, highlighting the areas which require specific attention for organisations already certified to BS 25999 and considering certification to ISO 22301.

Changing terminology
Reflecting the breadth of societal security, the ISO technical committee has introduced new terminology and you should remember to keep it in context with regional application of similar words. Some familiar terms used in BS 25999 have been replaced and these include:

- **Stakeholder** – now referred to as **Interested Party**
- **Preventive Action** – no longer used
- A new phrase **Action to address adverse trends or results before a non-conformity occurs** has been introduced
- **Critical Activities** – now replaced with **Prioritised Activities.**

As mentioned above, there are also several new and revised terms and definitions and you should read ISO 22300 to familiarise yourself with them.

Management system requirements
Greater emphasis is placed on some of the management system elements of the standard than in BS 25999. Not only has a new high level structure been introduced, but more attention has been placed on how the management system is

being operated and the expectation for it to be used to improve the organisation's BC arrangements. We will now consider the following management system changes:

- Top management responsibilities including BC objectives
- Actions to address risks and opportunities
- Awareness and communication
- Performance evaluation
- Improvement.

Top management responsibilities including BC objectives

(1) There is greater expectation for top management to get behind and support the BC policy. Through this statement of intent they must consider and express the purpose and direction of the organisation, rather than simply demonstrate commitment to the policy. In other words, they must consider the broader direction of the business when developing the policy and, with the new requirement for the policy to be made available to interested parties where authorised, the need for a cohesive message is significant.

(2) Greater visible leadership of the BCMS is expected. Demonstrable evidence of this will be how top management control the overall direction and operation of the BCMS, including through their communication of the policy and their support and encouragement to staff to maintain the integrity of the BCMS.

(3) Top management will appoint someone to be accountable for the entire BCMS rather than the BC policy and its implementation.

(4) Commitment to the BCMS is reinforced through a set of six requirements (**See ISO 22301 clause 5.2**). Whilst these are self explanatory, the requirement to 'ensure the BCMS achieves its expected outcomes' is interesting, not least because it requires top management to proactively assess the effectiveness of the BCMS against its set objectives. This should put a stop to rubber stamping a BCMS, which on occasion is witnessed by auditors. By itemising individual requirements, it helps to reinforce the importance of top management commitment to the BCMS.

(5) Responsibility for communicating and promoting the importance of meeting BCM objectives and complying with the BC policy now specifically rests with top management and not 'the organisation'.

(6) The organisation is required to set out its criteria for accepting risks as well as its acceptable levels of risk. This should help the organisation focus on its core business strategy and achieve its objectives whilst also monitoring for deviations from its accepted risk appetite. Previously, there was an implication that an organisation understood the level of risk it was prepared to accept and to use this as the basis for setting its BC objectives and establishing appropriate risk treatments. This was often found not to be the case by the auditor.

(7) Commitment to the exercise and test programme. This will encourage awareness, direct involvement where appropriate, and drive the improvement of BC arrangements. It will also demonstrate top management's commitment to the BCMS to staff and interested parties in a more tangible way.

(8) BC objectives remain a necessity and, to reinforce this point, now sit within their own clause heading. The requirements extend beyond purely setting objectives, and must be based on minimum product or service levels. They are specifically required to be measurable, have allocated responsibility and include a clear route map for their achievement.

Actions to address risks and opportunities

As part of the broader review of how management system standards are constructed, this new requirement is found in the **Planning** section of the standard.

The organisation is required to ascertain the risks and opportunities that need further consideration which, if left unaddressed, might prevent the BCMS from achieving its objectives. In other words, it will be expected to carry out a form of risk assessment on the BCMS itself and identify then implement corrective actions. The organisation must then review the effectiveness of these actions.

Awareness and communication

Previously documented under the heading 'Embedding BCM in the organisation's culture', **Awareness (ISO 22301 clause 7.3)** reaffirms the need for those under the control of the organisation to be aware of the BC policy and their contribution to the effectiveness of the BCMS. It goes further by stating that they will also be aware of the consequence of not meeting the requirements of the BCMS as well as their own role during a disruption. Methods by which to achieve this level of awareness are not specified, so the organisation must select the most appropriate for them.

The following clause, **7.4 Communication**, is new for ISO 22301. It requires the organisation to determine what and how BCMS communications will be managed for both internal and external parties, including the need to manage communications from interested parties. Methods of communication to be used during an incident also have to be identified and tested and could include alternative modes of communication not usually deployed by the organisation.

Performance evaluation

This ISO requirement appears different from that of 'Monitoring and Reviewing the BCMS' in BS 25999. Whilst the intent remains similar, more has been made of the need and importance of determining what performance metrics should be gathered in order to provide the best insight into the performance of the BCMS and whether it is meeting its objectives. Once again, methods are not specified and the organisation must choose the best ways to undertake this assessment, based on information available. For more information and guidance on this subject please refer to Appendix A.

Internal audit requirements have been extended to ensure best use is made of the audit findings, and reporting responsibilities are more explicit as is the ownership of corrective actions. Verification of follow up actions is also specified, demonstrating further intent by the standard to mandate ownership and responsibility of the BCMS.

Management review 'inputs' place greater emphasis on using information on BCMS performance to best effect and the 'outputs' extended to include procedural and control changes resulting from a reduction in risk or operations. The results of these reviews are to be communicated to interested parties deemed appropriate by the organisation.

Improvement

Nonconformities and corrective actions are the focus of this requirement and this is extended to their 'containment'. The organisation is expected to identify if and where similar nonconformities may have arisen elsewhere in the business and to implement corrective action. There is no longer a requirement for a documented procedure, and improvement will be based on objective measurement. This will be through the retention of information relating to the nature of nonconformities, subsequent actions and the results of these actions.

Continual improvement is required to the 'suitability' and 'adequacy' of the BCMS as well as its effectiveness.

TOP TIPS

The following tips are particularly aimed at those of you considering moving your BCMS from the requirements of BS 25999 to ISO 22301 and want to know the areas to focus on.

(1) To fully understand the breadth and approach adopted, read the complete series of ISO standards on BC.

(2) Provide sufficient information and support to your top management in order for them to fully understand and accept their BCMS role and responsibilities. Obtain assurance from them that they will actively participate in the BC programme.

(3) Review existing BC objectives to ensure that they meet the requirements of ISO 22301. Consider how you plan to achieve these objectives and who will be responsible for this. How will you verify this?

(4) Make sure that an outcome of the management review process is the clear assessment of current performance of the BCMS and whether it is achieving its objectives. This is not new but, with greater emphasis on this aspect of the BCMS, you may need to consider more proactive ways to demonstrate this.

(5) Make sure that local management are involved with internal audits of their areas of the business. They should be aware of findings and oversee subsequent action.

ACTION SHEET

Consider how you will use performance metrics to demonstrate the effectiveness of your BCMS. Be selective in what you measure and ensure a clear link back to the business strategy.

BCM requirements

Although the BCM requirements are broadly similar to that of BS 25999, there are some variances that require further thought. These are:

- Operational planning and control
- BIA and risk assessment
- BC strategies
- BC procedures
- Recovery
- Exercise and testing.

Operational planning and control

Planning your BC arrangements attracts greater focus in the international standard. In particular, the following requirements necessitate broader consideration:

- Understanding the needs and objectives of interested parties (linked to point below). This would include any regulatory requirements by which they are bound and also their needs, be they assumed or implied. ISO 22301 requires that any such legal or regulatory requirements, applicable to either the organisation or its interested parties, be identified, considered and documented for review purposes.

- The potential impact an incident might have on a interested party and on supply chains.

- The parameters for risk management; appetite, risk criteria and the purpose and scope of risk management activities, thus encouraging a more proactive approach to risk management.

- The retention of control over processes contracted out or outsourced (this may have been assumed before but not stipulated).

By incorporating the above areas into the planning phase of your BC arrangements you will be drawn to thinking not just about the needs of your own business but also those of interested parties. It should also encourage you to determine BC strategies that take into consideration the needs of others, which you may rely on before, during or after an incident.

BIA and risk assessment

Now under one clause heading, these two aspects of BC remain largely unchanged. To encourage consistency across BC arrangements the word **systematic** has been introduced. This particularly applies to defining how you evaluate potential impacts of an incident and how you assess and prioritise your risks, controls and treatments, and should encourage a uniformed approach by organisations.

The specified requirements for conducting a BIA have been reduced in number although the practical implications of this are limited. The main difference you will notice is that the terms maximum tolerable period of disruption (MTPD) and recovery time objective (RTO) no longer appear in the text. Instead, the following wording is used: '**setting prioritised timeframes for resuming these activities at a specified minimum acceptable level, taking into consideration the time within which the impacts of not resuming them would become unacceptable**'. However, both the aforementioned terms are included in the Terms and Definitions section of the standard.

The risk assessment requirements have been made more explicit to include supporting processes, systems, information, people and assets for prioritised activities. In addition, planning your risk management strategy is now more significant and this is extended to understanding the broader impact of those risks on regulatory requirements or society in general. Finally, treatments are linked back to the organisation's BC objectives and risk appetite. All of which should result in a more considered risk assessment process.

BC strategies

The strategies your organisation chooses shall reflect the findings of the BIA and risk assessment. This requirement has not changed. Once suitable options have been identified, you now have a list of suggested resource requirements which will help you decide what is needed to achieve these strategies. The standard clearly states that the list is not exhaustive so make sure that you consider resources that might be pertinent to your organisation but not necessarily listed.

BC procedures

ISO 22301 lays out the requirements for developing a response differently from BS 25999. Under the heading 'BC Procedures' we not only find the requirements for response but also for 'Warning and communication'. ISO 22301 encourages a proactive approach to considering the impacts caused by a **potential** disruption as well as how this might be communicated to interested parties.

The incident response requirements are broadly similar with a few exceptions. There is a new expectation that the organisation will have identified the trigger point (referred to as 'impact threshold') for invocation of the plan or response and to consider the circumstances under which it might communicate externally about its risks and impacts.

A new requirement under clause **8.4.3 Warning and communication** has been added to ensure that the organisation has established procedures for detecting, monitoring and communicating news of incidents to interested parties, including internally. This clause provides detailed guidelines to be followed and will ensure that you consider carefully what actions are required, by whom, before and in the event of a disruption. You should read this clause in detail and fully consider what is required.

Overall, the content of BC plans remain largely unchanged from BS 25999. However, the requirements for each plan, as opposed to collectively, have been extended and now include plan objectives, invocation and implementation procedures, communication requirements and procedures, interdependencies and interactions and resource needs. You should review your existing plans and make the necessary changes to ensure that they reflect the new requirements.

Recovery

The international standard indicates that the recovery of an organisation requires the transition from its temporary state of operation back to normal business functionality. This may cause confusion amongst practitioners as the requirement might otherwise be known as resumption. (Refer to The BCI's *Good Practice Guidelines 2010 for more details*.) Resumption did not overtly form part of the requirements in BS 25999.

We need to ask ourselves how far the standard expects us to reasonably go in determining back-to-normal operations and indeed what 'back to normal' might look like after an incident.

Exercise and testing

The intent and methods used to exercise and test BCM arrangements remain unchanged, as is the need to conduct them at planned intervals. However, the need for an approved **programme** of exercises and tests has been removed. This is curious as it makes good business sense to have a programme which top management have signed up to, as well as providing a useful prompter to discuss the related costs, and you should consider how you will address this point in the future.

TOP TIPS

(1) It is all in the preparation. Make sure you spend plenty of time planning your BC arrangements. Be able to demonstrate the reasoning behind your decisions and how you have considered the needs and expectations of interested parties.

(2) Ensure the organisation's risk appetite is understood and be ready to justify this. Remember that your appetite for risk may change as a result of circumstances both within and beyond your control, so be flexible to change.

(3) Working systematically, your organisation will be well placed to understand its business and apply solutions that reflect its core needs and those of interested parties.

(4) Determine what 'recovery' means to your organisation and how you intend to demonstrate this through your BCM arrangements. You should be in control of setting suitable boundaries.

ACTION SHEET

Consider the human aspects of your continuity strategies. Taking into account the findings of your BIA and risk assessment, list below what you need to include when preparing a strategy for the organisation's most important resource, its staff.

You may find it helpful to refer to PD 25111:2010 *Business Continuity Management Guidance on Human Aspects of Business Continuity.*

ACTION SHEET

Take time to review your existing BC plans and compare the existing format and contents to the requirements of ISO 22301. List below what you need to change or add to them.

CERTIFICATE TRANSITION

Organisations which are certified or in the process of becoming certified to an existing BC standard such as BS 25999 need to decide whether they wish to become certified to ISO 22301.

The transition process

Your certification body will provide details of how they will transition clients from one standard to another. Based on the differences between BS 25999 and ISO 22301, this is likely to be achieved through the normal surveillance audit programme[11]. Time will be allocated during these audits to focus on the new requirements of ISO 22301 and evidence sought to support whether or not the organisation meets these requirements.

---

[11] Additional audits may be required where, for example, major issues remain outstanding and extra time is considered necessary to address these and the new requirements.

Once all these requirements have been assessed and judged as being met, the auditor will be in a position to recommend certification to the new standard (subject to the certification body's usual independent review process), and your organisation will have completed the transition process upon receipt of a new certificate.

The following questions and answers may help you select the best option for your organisation.

Q. What does transitioning mean?
A. An organisation which currently holds a certificate, for example to BS 25999-2, may choose to transfer its certification to the new international standard ISO 22301. To achieve this, certain additional requirements will have to be met and approved by a certification body.

Q. How long does it take to transfer from one standard to another?
A. This will depend on two principle factors: the extent of the differences between the two standards described in this book and the structure and operation of the existing BCMS. Guidance should be given by your certification body.

Q. Does my organisation have to transfer its registration from one standard to another?
A. No. Your organisation may decide to retain its certification to the existing BC standard and not seek certification to ISO 22301. In this case, certification will remain valid for as long as the existing standard continues to be recognised as a specification standard and is auditable by the certification body. You should seek further advice from your existing certification body.

Q. Can my organisation be certified to more than one BCMS standard?
A. Yes. For as long as your certification body continues to offer certification to the existing standard, you may retain your certificate (subject to the normal audit programme requirements). If your organisation wishes to be certified to ISO 22301 as well this is possible but your BCMS would need to meet all additional requirements before achieving certification. Because of the cost implications of this option, careful consideration should be given to the reasons why multiple certifications might be advantageous to your organisation.

The role of the accreditation body
An accreditation body is responsible for providing guidance and instruction to certification bodies about the transition process from one standard to another. To do this, it considers the new standards' requirements and determines what the certification bodies should do to offer certification services to the new standard. Guidance on timescales for transitioning between standards will also be provided.

The role of the certification body
Once instruction has been received from the accreditation body, the certification body will review its existing scheme requirements and make any necessary changes. This is likely to involve additional training for auditors and possibly a revision to audit requirements.

In order for certification bodies to be able to offer accredited certification services to ISO 22301 they must successfully pass an assessment by their accreditation body. This includes certification bodies already accredited to BS 25999. Those not seeking accreditation may offer unaccredited certification services to the new standard.

If it is your organisation's intention to become certified to ISO 22301, you should speak to your selected certification body as soon as possible (refer to Chapter 5 Choosing a certification body). They will provide you with the information required to plan for this event.

ACTION SHEET

Write down here any actions that your organisation needs to take if it is considering the transition to ISO 22301. Add suggested time lines against each action and discuss them with your certification body as well as your BC sponsor.

SUMMARY

(1) The proposed new structure to Management System Standard requirements will help organisations with multiple systems streamline their processes.

(2) Top management will be required to proactively demonstrate commitment to the BCMS.

(3) Select methods of reviewing BCMS performance carefully in order to obtain valuable information about the suitability, adequacy and effectiveness of the BCMS.

(4) Share the outcomes of the BCMS performance reviews and use them to improve the management system.

(5) Greater planning of your BCMS will lead to better business continuity preparedness.

(6) Approach the transition to ISO 22301 in a methodical way and understand how your certification body intends to facilitate this.

5 THE CERTIFICATION PROCESS

PURPOSE AND OBJECTIVE

The purpose of this chapter is to explain the certification process and to provide an insight into the different phases of the audit programme and how to prepare for it. We will also discuss what you should consider in order to maintain momentum after certification. The objective is to equip organisations that are seeking certification with the appropriate information before they commit to the application process.

TERMS AND DEFINITIONS

Accreditation: The formal acknowledgement bestowed upon a certification body by an accreditation body that it has demonstrated compliance to internationally recognised standards (most notably BS EN ISO/IEC 17021:2011 and BS EN ISO 19011:2011).

Accreditation Body: Formally recognised organisation which assesses the capability of a certification body against international standards to demonstrate their competence, impartiality and performance capability.

Audit: systematic, independent and documented process for obtaining audit evidence and evaluating it objectively to determine the extent to which the audit criteria are fulfilled[12].

Certification: The formal acknowledgement by a certification body that an organisation has demonstrated compliance to a particular management system standard.

Certification Body: A third party organisation offering management system assessment certification services to organisations.

---

[12] An audit can be an internal audit (first party) or an external audit (second party or third party), and it can be a combined audit (combining two or more disciplines). 'Audit evidence' and 'audit criteria' are defined in ISO 19011 (Source: ISO 22301:2012).

An example to help explain the above, often miss applied terminology, would be:

XYZ Ltd applies for certification to ISO 22301 through a certification body. The certification body will provide the third party assessment service and, upon demonstration by XYZ Ltd that they have complied with the requirements of ISO 22301 by way of an audit or audits, will grant XYZ Ltd certification to the standard. The certification body may in turn, wish to be accredited by, for example, The United Kingdom Accreditation Service (UKAS) and will have to be independently assessed by UKAS in order to demonstrate their own compliance to internationally recognised standards. NOTE: Not being accredited does not prohibit a certification body from offering (unaccredited) certification services to its clients.

CHOOSING A CERTIFICATION BODY

It is very important when choosing a certification body to consider a number of factors. In order to get the most from your working relationship with a certification body it should be that of a partnership between both parties. At no time should you feel under pressure or not in control of your audit programme.

Certification bodies may provide both accredited and unaccredited certification services. To be able to provide an accredited certification service, the certification body will need to have undergone its own 'audit' with an accreditation body. It must demonstrate compliance to internationally recognised standards and demonstrate its competence, impartiality and performance capability. Achieving accreditation enables the certification body to show that it has passed tough scrutiny and therefore provides a high degree of professional comfort to its customers. Some certification bodies may be accredited to some standards and not others. This may be of their own choosing and is an area you should discuss with them as part of your selection process.

Selecting a certification body, that has or has not obtained accreditation to the standard you are seeking to become certified to, is your organisation's choice. However, there may be external factors that influence your decision. These could include:

- Specific customer or supplier expectations and requirements
- Tendering stipulations
- Competitor pressure.

Any of these additional requirements could effectively make the decision for you and, if this is the case, you still have a choice of certification bodies to choose from.

Here are some additional areas for you to consider when selecting your preferred certification body:

- If the accreditation status of your certification body is important, this should be your first point of enquiry as it will eliminate some certification bodies immediately.

- Does your organisation have any existing management system standard certifications? If so, which certification body are they with? Does your company wish to continue with the same body or are they happy to work with more than one body?

- By obtaining a number of quotations from various bodies you will get a feel for which organisation you lean towards. Style of auditing and client management may vary as will costs and the structure of charges and your decision should be a balance of these factors.

- Do you have a preference towards building a working relationship with a specific auditor in order for them to become familiar with your organisation and management system, or would you prefer to maintain a more individual approach by having a variety of auditors? Each approach has its pros and cons and you should discuss this with the certification bodies that you meet with as they may allocate auditors in different ways.

AUDIT STAGES

The certification process is made up of various stages (see Figure 5.1). Some stages are linked to the initial achievement of a standard and others to maintaining certification once it has been awarded. All are mandatory and the certification body will have recommended time lines between each stage.

Figure 5.1 Audit stages

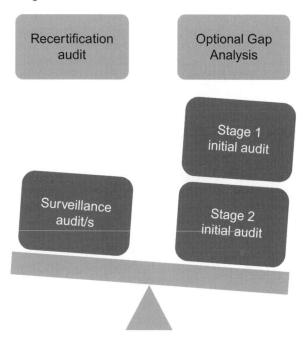

77

The duration of each audit stage is based on a number of factors, typically the scope of the BCMS selected, the size and complexity of the 'scoped' organisation and the number of staff employed at each location within the scope.

Initial audit

The initial audit will generally be undertaken in two phases and might be referred to as Stage 1 and Stage 2 initial audits. The reason for this is so the certification body can focus on different aspects of the management system as well as different levels of implementation during each audit.

Stage 1 will typically consider the documentation requirements and assess the organisation's understanding of the requirements of the standard. It will assess the methods of implementation as well as the management system control elements, such as the internal audit and management review processes, and any documented procedures. The aim of the stage 1 audit is to establish the current level of conformance of the system and to gauge the level of readiness to move forward to the next phase of the initial audit. It will also form part of the planning process for the stage 2 initial audit. The duration of this phase of the initial audit is likely to be less than the second phase.

Stage 2 will focus more heavily on the implementation of BCM methodologies and how effective these are in achieving the BC objectives. It will involve sampling the various documents and resources involved and to assess whether the performance information collated is being used in such a way as to improve the BCMS. Ultimately, it will seek to verify what has been observed during the stage 1 audit and to demonstrate to the auditor that the BCMS is sufficiently robust to be effective. Of course, compliance with the requirements of the standard is also necessary.

Assuming a reasonable level of compliance is found during the stage 1 audit, the timeline between stages 1 and 2 is likely to be between 2–4 months. Based on the findings during stage 1, it may be necessary for the organisation to carry out further preparation work in order to move forward to stage 2. If readiness for stage 2 falls outside six months, it is not unusual for the certification body to request a further stage 1 audit before proceeding further with certification.

Surveillance audit

The purpose of the surveillance audit is for the certification body to ensure the organisation is maintaining its BCMS in line with the requirements of the standard in between recertification audits. Not all aspects of the BCMS will necessarily be assessed during each surveillance visit but the aim of the certification body will be to have assessed all elements between periods of recertification. However, there are some elements of the BCMS that will be audited on every occasion. These will include internal audits, management review meetings and any changes to the BCMS itself based on changes to the scope or business risks.

Expect your certification body to provide you with a programme of what they plan to audit and when during the audit cycle, as part of the stage 2 audit. The frequency of surveillance audits will depend on a number of factors and will be confirmed by the certification body at the end of the initial audit process. It is most likely to be either at six or twelve monthly intervals.

The total duration of surveillance visits carried out between recertification audits will depend on their frequency. However, they will usually equate to approximately the same number of days as made up the combined stage 1 and 2 initial audits. For example:

XYZ Ltd has an initial audit, made up of a stage 1 of two days and stage 2 of six days. Surveillance visits are to be carried out annually and each surveillance visit will be in the order of four days. NOTE: These durations may alter if there are shifts or a high number of staff undertaking the same or similar roles.

Health warning

Failure to demonstrate that your BCMS remains compliant and fit for purpose may result in the withdrawal of your certificate. However, this will not be done without your certification body first issuing you with a warning and the opportunity to rectify omissions.

Recertification audit

Most certification bodies now issue certificates to International and British Standards with an expiry date of three years from the date of original certification. Recertification is required **prior** to this expiry date.

The purpose of the recertification audit is for the certification body to confirm the continuing capability of the organisation to meet all the requirements of the standard. Assuming this is the case, certification will be maintained. The recertification audit will cover the entire scope of the BCMS, as for the combined stage 1 and 2 initial audits, and will not only look for compliance but also that the BCMS is continuing to improve and develop in line with your business requirements, taking into consideration any internal or external changes.

Gap analysis

Whilst these standalone assessments are outside the formal remit of the certification process, they are often considered to be crucial in order for the organisation to understand how its BCMS compares to the requirements of the standard. The gap analysis may be undertaken purely for internal purposes or to assess the readiness to proceed with certification. The findings are not formally carried forward to the initial audit phase.

Gap Analyses are offered by certification bodies and external consultancy firms alike. If you intend to have one, you should consider where you are likely to get most value from. A certification body will treat the gap analysis as an informal audit and benchmark you against the standard, identifying gaps where appropriate. A consultant will carry out a similar review and will also be able to provide advice where further attention is required, something which management system auditors are prohibited from doing.

You should view a gap analysis as an investment in the development of your BCMS. Whilst there is a cost involved, this should be weighed against the potential peace of mind such a review offers. Consider the effect on staff morale, not to mention management objectives, if, by not having gone through a gap analysis, nonconformities are left undiscovered until the initial audit and, as a result, you fail to achieve certification. The costs incurred, time lost and downbeat message received by the business could be very damaging to the ongoing success of your BCMS.

Audit checklist
The checklist at Table 5.1 will provide you with an idea of the areas that will be audited during the stage 1 and 2 initial audits. It will help you plan for your audits and be prepared for what to expect. However, it is not an exhaustive list and your certification body should provide an audit plan prior to each audit phase.

You will notice there appears to be a high degree of repetition between audit stages 1 and stage 2. This is because the purpose of the stage 1 audit is to establish

Table 5.1 Audit checklist

Requirement	Stage 1	Stage 2
BCMS scope	✓	✓
BC policy and objectives	✓	✓
BCMS manual/documentation	✓	✓
BCMS procedures	✓	✓
Resources	✓	✓
Competencies	✓	✓
Management commitment		✓
Communication and consultation	✓	✓
BCMS awareness		✓
BIA	✓	✓
Risk assessment	✓	✓
BC strategies	✓	✓
BC procedures	✓	✓
BC plans	✓	✓
Exercise and test	✓	✓
Internal audit	✓	✓
Management review	✓	✓
Monitoring, measurement, analysis and evaluation		✓
Actions and improvement	✓	✓

arrangements have been put in place and stage 2 is to test these arrangements for their effectiveness. Depending on the level of compliance observed during the stage 1 audit, some areas may not need to be reviewed again if perhaps there are no additional auditors joining the team at stage 2 or no further action has been taken by the organisation since stage 1.

For example, how stage 1 and 2 audits might approach the subject of 'Competence': ISO 22301 defines competence as 'ability to apply knowledge and skills to achieve intended results'. ISO 22301 requires that 'the organisation shall,

(a) determine the necessary competence of person(s) doing work under its control that affects its performance;

(b) ensure these persons are competent on the basis of appropriate education, training, and experience;

(c) where applicable, take actions to acquire the necessary competence, and evaluate the effectiveness of the actions taken[13];

(d) retain appropriate documented information as evidence of competence.

Stage 1 audit requirements
The auditor will seek evidence to demonstrate that a method of determining the necessary competencies has been considered and implemented which, in turn, has resulted in the identification of suitable resource to undertake the activities required. These activities should also be clearly identified. The achievement, or route to achievement, of these competencies will need to be identified.

There is a requirement for a system to record how competencies are to be achieved along with a method for determining the effectiveness of this process. Finally, a record of achievement of competencies, or the route towards such achievement, is expected. In other words, that all of the building blocks are in place.

Stage 2 audit requirements
Here, the auditor will want to see the building blocks are actually built up in such a way that can demonstrate not only that they conform to the requirements of the standard but are also actually giving you the results you need in order to have suitably competent staff in the right place and performing their role in an appropriate and effective manner.

An example here might be that Joe has been identified as the most suitable person to manage the development of the company's BIA. To support this decision it is known that during his previous employment, Joe was involved in a similar process, but as someone who had only input into the overall BIA process. In order to make sure Joe has the right competency-set to enable him to manage this process now, his manager decides to send him on a training course, provided by a specialist third party provider where he will learn how to develop a BIA using different tools and methods. Once Joe has completed his training (for which he will obtain a certificate)

---

[13] Applicable actions can include, for example, the provision of training to, the mentoring of, or the re-assignment of current employees; or the hiring or contracting of competent persons.

he will start work on the new BIA process. His performance will be monitored by his line manager and BC manager and an evaluation made of his ability to carry out the task of developing the BIA for the business. Suitable records will be maintained and made available to the auditor, and Joe will be available to speak to the auditor about his training and subsequent work experience.

Finally, the ultimate proof of Joe's competency level will be in a review of the BIA itself to ensure the process adopted has resulted in a compliant BIA which is fit for its intended purpose.

ACTION SHEET

Having reviewed the audit checklist, make a list of actions you feel are still required in order to meet the requirements of both stages of the initial audit.

TOP TIP

Do not under estimate the degree of implementation you will need to demonstrate during both stages of the initial audit. Make sure you are using your BCMS in earnest before the audit process. The more developed your BCMS at the time of the stage 1 audit, the better you will be able to prove the robustness of your system controls.

WHAT TO EXPECT FROM THE AUDIT PROCESS

Once you have submitted the application to your chosen certification body, they should allocate the appropriate audit resource for your forthcoming audits. This auditor should be your main point of contact from then on.

Accredited certification bodies must all operate their management system audit services in line with certain standards. This is what you should rightfully expect:

- To function in an organised and open manner and one that encourages a partnership approach throughout the duration of the professional relationship;

- Impartiality of both the certification body and auditor;

- Confidentiality between parties at all times;

- A competent auditor who has suitable industry sector experience;

- Clear lines of communication;

- Mutually agreed audit dates;

- Audit plan available prior to each audit;

- Opening and closing audit meetings which cover the critical aspects of the audit process and answer any remaining questions about the audit protocols;

- Open discussions during the audit with no surprises at the end;

- A clearly written and balanced report which provides details of any actions required as a result of the audit findings.

TOP TIP

If you do not hear from the auditor within a reasonable timeframe, initiate contact with them and ask them to provide details of the forthcoming audit. Remember, you need to maintain control over the audit process so it moves in the direction you want it to.

HOW TO PREPARE FOR THE AUDIT

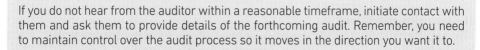

Say what you do, do what you say and then prove it.

This is the best piece of advice I could give to anyone who is about to embark on establishing a BCMS. It sounds so simple and taken literally, will satisfy the auditor.

Say what you do by either producing a documented procedure or defined methodology, as is either required by the standard or considered most appropriate for the format of your BCMS. Be clear, concise and make sure it accurately reflects what you are doing. Where appropriate, try to explain the reasoning behind the approach taken.

Do what you say means just that. You cannot be surprised if the auditor picks you up for doing something in a different way from that documented. To remain compliant, you must remember to amend your procedures, and other documents, should what you do change (for any reason). For example, if a new piece of legislation is introduced which has an impact on your business, you must have a system in place to ensure such changes are picked up and included within your procedures.

Prove it. Writing down what you do is only the start of implementing a BCMS. Not unreasonably, you will be asked to prove that what you say is actually what you do.

Proof may be defined as 'the evidence or argument establishing a fact or the truth of a statement' (Source: Oxford English Dictionary). This 'proof' can be in various forms and it is down to you to decide what is appropriate. If you can answer yes to the following criteria, the auditor should accept it:

- Does it demonstrate the performance of an act or process?
- Is it current?
- Is it relevant?
- Is it in a suitable format?
- Can it be repeated and sustained?

Knowing what the auditor expects in terms of proof is a constant concern to those being audited. What you need to remember is that it is your system, run by you, for your business needs, and the proof or evidence of this must come from you. The role of the auditor is to interpret the evidence and to determine compliance (or not).

The provision of evidence
The requirement to provide evidence of the fulfilment of specific aspects of your BCMS (outputs) prior to assessing their effectiveness is far more pronounced in the ISO standard. This puts the onus on the organisation to prove the productivity of its BCMS rather than straight forward compliance.

Remember that, as ISO 22301 is a specification standard, the evidence should be auditable. Audit evidence is defined as 'records, statements of fact or other information, which are relevant to the audit criteria and verifiable'[14].

The Types of Evidence list offers some suggestions of the sort of evidence the auditor will be looking for.

---

[14] Audit evidence may be qualitative or quantitative. (Source: BS EN ISO 19011:2011 Guidelines for auditing management systems).

- Reports (e.g. incident, exercise, test, performance analysis, audit);

- Meeting minutes (preferably with clear allocation of actions and timelines where appropriate);

- Email confirmations (e.g. approving or accepting something);

- Contracts/service level agreements;

- Presentation slides (e.g. to top management);

- Training material and training certificates (and other qualification records);

- BCM documentation (e.g. BIA, risk register, BC plans) and BCMS documentation (e.g. policy, BCMS procedures).

How long you should retain evidence is a matter for your organisation to determine. Consideration should be given as to whether:

- You will be required to produce the information for internal and/or external auditors;

- Stakeholders will expect to see specific evidence for example results of exercises or incident reports;

- Regulatory and/or contractual requirements dictate particular timescales.

Self assess your BCMS
As part of your preparation for certification you should undertake some form of self assessment of your system, procedures and processes. After all, you would not go to an exam without revising for it and being as confident as possible you had covered the syllabus! A BCMS audit is no different, and the objective is to be able to demonstrate to the auditor that you have addressed all the requirements of the standard and you have confidence in your system's ability to perform effectively.

There are several products on the market that will 'help' you to assess your level of compliance with the standard and, in some cases, flag up issues which need to be addressed. These often come at a price, and you should think carefully about what you want from the tool before committing yourself to any one in particular. After all, the best tool you could have is a copy of the standard (and this handbook, of course) and the instinctive ability to judge whether you have met the requirements. Where you identify gaps, you need to give yourself sufficient time to address these and then reassess the requirement based on the actions taken to ensure that you now comply with that particular requirement.

Appendix B provides a self assessment checklist.

TOP TIP

Once you have identified what evidence will be relied upon to support the fulfilment of BCMS requirements, consider how and where you will store this information. It will make your life much easier when it comes to being audited (both internally and externally). Whilst not a new requirement, it is surprising how often 'key' evidence such as management decisions, cannot be located when required.

Is the workforce engaged?

Asking your staff to take on new things can be challenging and you need to be able to sell the benefits to them. This task will be made considerably easier if you have the support and backing of top management. Your management team should champion the BCMS and proactively demonstrate their commitment to it.

With the support of top management, you need to ensure that everyone who is covered by the scope of your BCMS (and potentially beyond), has sufficient aware-ness and understanding of how BC affects the organisation, themselves and their ability to carry on doing their job. This awareness may be anything from knowing or having access to the employee emergency phone number to ring, or being involved in an exercise, to a high level of practical knowledge of what the most time-critical activities are within the organisation. Whoever your target audience is, you will need to ensure that messages and other communications issued to the workforce are relevant, clear and timely. In other words, you tailor the communications and exercises to the people who will be receiving them and you choose carefully how and when you do this so as not to over burden them with information whilst maintain-ing a level of relevant information.

As far as the audit is concerned, the auditor will expect to see that you have rolled out your BCMS to everyone within the selected scope. They are likely to test the effectiveness of this by selecting different people from a sample of departments and locations and speaking with them directly. This will be covered in more detail later in this chapter but, in terms of preparing for the audit, you need to be as confident as possible that all staff, no matter who they are or what they do, have an appropriate level of BCMS awareness. Include this as part of your self assessment process and walk around the departments and speak to staff about their experience with the BCMS. Typically, you would expect all staff to have the following basic knowledge of the BCMS:

- What BC means and why the organisation has plans in place to reduce the impact of a disruption;

- That a BC policy exists and that the organisation has set itself BC objectives (detailed knowledge of these objectives is not necessary for all staff);

- Where BCMS procedures are located for reference purposes (for example the company intranet);

- How, in the event of a business disruption, their job role would be affected and what they would be expected to do and/or where to go during this time;

- How their day-to-day activities may be impacted and reprioritised in the event of a business disruption;

- Personal experience of a BC exercise, its purpose and outcome.

Fools rush in

As part of your preparation for certification, you will need to assess your state of readiness for the audit. It is not uncommon for organisations to have an anticipated timeline by which to achieve certification and this can often be quite demanding. This deadline may be driven by external forces such as customer requirements but you need to be realistic when setting these timeframes and recognise that a flexible approach is necessary. Ultimately, if you rush through the implementation of the BCMS you risk damaging your chances of a successful outcome from the audit.

Another point to consider is that systems take time to settle down and become 'the norm' within an organisation. Would you launch a new IT system into your business without the proper testing? No. So do not launch your BCMS the week before the audit is due to take place. Allow enough time for staff to gain an understanding of the BCMS, see the results of some exercises and possibly be part of an internal audit. I talked about having sufficient evidence to support the management of the BCMS, and a further example of this would be having run a few management review meetings and internal audits and being able to provide evidence of the outcomes of these.

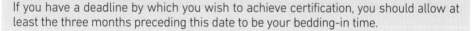

TOP TIP

If you have a deadline by which you wish to achieve certification, you should allow at least the three months preceding this date to be your bedding-in time.

ACTION SHEET

Having reviewed the suggested evidence list and undertaken your self assessment, make a list of the evidence that you will draw upon to demonstrate the effectiveness of your BCMS to the auditor.

THE AUDIT EXPERIENCE

'My only fear is the unknown.'

David Blaine, Illusionist

An audit of any kind can be a daunting prospect, especially if it is the first time you have been through such an event. The fear of the unknown and the anticipation that you might say or do something wrong can sometimes be overwhelming, and the effects on personnel should not be underestimated.

Thankfully, at least with management system audits, we are moving past the days when an auditor would approach an audit with a tick-box mentality, where the client had to pass each requirement before moving to the next one. It is true that you must still demonstrate compliance to the requirements of the standard, but how you do this is a little less prescriptive now and the onus is on you to satisfy the auditor and their line of questioning. In essence, there is a partnership approach to management system audits and the auditor's role is to look for compliance rather than noncompliance.

Managing expectations

It is true that if someone understands the reason behind an action or decision, they are more likely to accept it. The same can be said of an audit. If you take time to meet with staff and explain about the audit process the organisation is about to go through, this should help them prepare for it as individuals.

Your discussion could include the following points:

- Why the organisation has sought to become certified to the standard;
- The focus of the audit will be on BC processes and how they are carried out by the business;
- The audit will not focus on individual performance but the overall effectiveness of the BCMS;
- Share the audit agenda with staff so they know when to expect the auditor;
- A question and answer session for staff to raise their own questions and concerns.

Who should represent the organisation during the audit?

It is really important to make sure that you have the right people representing the company and this includes management. By this I mean those with the most relevant expertise and involvement in the BCMS and, of course, the sponsor or management team responsible for endorsing the BCMS. The audit is your opportunity to show how well you have done and that your confidence in the BCMS is well founded. This will be done best by people who are familiar with its development and testing. Make sure that, as part of the audit planning process, everyone's diaries are freed up for at least some of the audit duration, checking with the auditor in advance how long each session is likely to last if you need to.

In particular, you should explain to top management that they may be invited to a discussion with the auditor. A good way of understanding how an organisation operates is to ask the top management team and then follow their answers through the organisation to see if what they perceive to be their message is actually the one received by staff. Typically, the auditor will be interested to understand management's involvement with BC and how the BC policy and objectives have been linked to the organisation's overall strategic plan. This will then lead on to more detailed questions and the aim is to determine how engaged the management team is with the BCMS.

Demonstrating continual improvement

The aim of any management system is to develop the most appropriate recurring activities to enhance performance. This may take some time and you will learn through experience what works best for your organisation. The auditor understands that perfection does not usually happen the first time of doing something and will expect to see that you have systems in place to ensure that lessons are learned and improvements made as part of your BCMS journey. This is a useful message to relay to staff so that they too understand that it is a progressive journey that the organisation is on.

The audit team

The size of the audit team selected by the certification body will be based primarily on the scope and extent of your BCMS. Factors that will have been taken into consideration will include the number of locations included, the number of staff at each location and the complexity of operations at each location.

Whilst every application to a certification body is different, a typical audit which covers one or two locations within a reasonable travelling distance from each other may only demand a single auditor. However, where greater distances are involved between locations (and this could include different countries), a team of auditors will be allocated. Within this team, a lead auditor will be appointed and it is their responsibility to act as coordinator for the other auditors and to manage the entire audit process. This will include the assessment of findings and final recommendation decision. Within the audit team there will be auditors who have experience of the relevant industry sector as well as BCMSs. In the event that a trainee auditor forms part of the team, they will usually be shadowed by a more experienced auditor. Auditors will generally work independently of each other apart from the opening and closing meeting formalities and some specific audit areas. However, the lead auditor will ensure that findings from the audit team are shared amongst themselves during the audit, in order for any trends (good or bad) and concerns to be highlighted. This could potentially lead to further investigation by the audit team to determine whether or not a deeper problem exists across the organisation.

Where distance plays a part in the audit logistics, it is not unusual for teleconferences to be held in order to share information and attend joint meetings, for example with senior management.

The audit plan

The auditor/lead auditor will prepare a plan for the forthcoming audit. This should provide you with sufficient detail in order to be able to plan time in people's diaries, as is required. If you find that there is a clash of commitments at your end, you should ask the auditor to move the plan timings around where possible. There is generally a degree of flexibility with the audit plan and even last minute changes should be able to be accommodated.

Where the audit is across a number of locations, the plan should include each location. This will enable you to see which auditor will visit which site, when, and what areas of the BCMS they intend to cover. It is then up to you to ensure that each location has appointed a representative who will be responsible for the auditor whilst they are on site. This would include the usual health and safety requirements for visitors, however, if some or all of your locations have visitor induction procedures or other specific health and safety requirements because of the nature of the environment being visited, the auditor will expect to undertake these.

The audit plan will be based on a sampling approach. On account of the limited amount of time an auditor spends with a client, they have to collect examples of functions, processes and plans as they do not have sufficient time to necessarily look at everything. The information gathered must be relevant to the audit and verifiable. In other words, the evidence collected must corroborate (or not) that the requirements of the standard are being met. The basis of the sampling will normally be discussed with you beforehand so that the auditor is sure that they have made an appropriate selection across the scope of the BCMS. However, you should be aware that it is up to the auditor to select this sample and not you and some areas to be sampled may not be selected until the time of the audit. This will ensure that an independent audit takes place.

Example of how a sample may be selected during an ISO 22301 initial audit

As part of their BCMS implementation, a company has developed ten functional BIA's plus three for the relevant support services. This information has subsequently been consolidated into an overarching BIA.

A companywide risk assessment process has been established which incorporates risks identified as part of the BCMS.

There is one incident management plan and eight BC plans. The sample selected might look like this:

- Three function based BIAs selected by their level of priority to the company's key products or services;

- Up to three support service BIAs, depending on the criticality of service they provide, for example IT, HR, procurement, finance;

- The overarching BIA in order to track through how the low level BIA information has been transferred and translated;

- The risk assessment register (or as appropriate) to track how prioritised activities have been risk assessed, evaluated and treated;

- The incident management plan and three BC plans, likely to be from those following on from the BIAs sampled.

Raising audit findings

During the audit, the auditor may decide to raise issues which they feel require attention or further consideration. These findings are based on varying levels of severity and may have no, little or significant impact on the outcome of the audit. Whilst the terminology amongst certification bodies tends to vary a little, the basis of the findings can be categorised as follows:

Observation: an area of the BCMS which might benefit from further thought and development of procedure or process.

Example: A corrective action log already exists and this could be adapted to include BCMS actions.

Nonconformity: an area of the BCMS which does not comply with a requirement of the standard. It may be a single lapse or there may be evidence of a few lapses but in isolation, the nonconformity does not render the BCMS ineffective.

Example: The BC policy does not provide the framework for setting business continuity objectives or include a commitment to the continual improvement of the BCMS.

Major nonconformity: an area or areas which show that there has been a breakdown in the implementation of the BCMS in accordance with the requirements of the standard. The severity of which will preclude the auditor from being able to make a positive recommendation for certification until suitable corrective action has been undertaken and verified.

Example: No BCMS internal audit schedule has been produced and no audits conducted to date. No competent internal auditor has been selected.

Audit reporting

An important part of the audit process is the report that the auditor will produce once they have completed the audit itself. Notes and findings identified during the audit will be consolidated into a report, which is ideally completed on site as part of the audit agenda. Most certification bodies expect their auditors to provide both verbal feedback and, wherever possible, a written report before the audit concludes. The audit report is typically generated electronically.

Audit reports are expected to include certain information, not least a summary of the audit findings, details of the findings raised under each applicable category and any further action required by the client. Where the audit is due to provide a certification recommendation, this will also be written in the report. Details of the next audit may also be outlined in the report to assist with future planning. The style and level of content in reports does vary considerably and this, in part, is down to the auditor's individual style of commentary. If for any reason you consider that the report presented to you does not accurately reflect the audit discussions and findings, then you should make this known to the auditor. You should also ensure that you fully understand the commentary and in particular the expectation from actions required to rectify any nonconformities. You should do this as soon as possible, whilst the audit discussions are still fresh in your mind.

Some auditors issue reports in draft to allow the client to read it through and confirm acceptance, others will only provide the client with a final version.

After the audit
If the audit has resulted in a certification decision being made, an independent review of the report will be made by the certification body's review team. This will ensure that the audit plan was appropriate and the requirements of the standard have been fully covered during the audit. It will also ensure that the auditor's recommendation for certification (or not) was appropriate. It is only after this review has been undertaken that you will be formally notified of the result and (hopefully) receive your certificate. A similar review will be undertaken as part of recertification audits but certification bodies may undertake additional internal reviews as part of their ongoing training, development and compliance requirements.

MAINTAINING MOMENTUM AFTER THE INITIAL AUDIT AND BETWEEN AUDITS

Achieving certification is only the start of your BCMS journey. It takes an equal amount of energy and focus (if not more) to maintain momentum once you have become certified. It is not unusual for organisations to let their attention slip for a few months whilst they are still basking in their initial success, knowing that the auditors will not be back for some time. If this timeframe is allowed to creep, people's attention may move to other business requirements and all the good work done to achieve certification could begin to suffer.

I should also point out that what we discuss in this chapter can be applied to organisations which have not opted for certification, but which still operate a BCMS.

How to remain focused
The sooner you adopt a programme of self evaluation and performance reviews, the easier it will be for you to maintain awareness and buy-in for your BCMS, across the organisation. If staff see that the BC manager has taken his eye off the ball, they will assume that it is okay for them to do so as well. You will need the support of your senior management team in order to introduce these initiatives.

Some ideas of how to keep your BCMS fresh, both for individuals and as an organisation are in Table 5.2.

Table 5.2 Maintaining focus

Maintaining individual awareness	Maintaining organisational focus
Try and ensure that your BCM exercise programme extends to every member of staff within a 12 month period.	Make sure that feedback from exercises is communicated throughout the business and attention is paid to how the 'organisation' performed.
As part of the ongoing embedding programme, encourage individuals to participate in company run BCM related activities.	To encourage an organisational culture of 'continual improvement', identify ways to improve future exercises and tests and communicate these to the business.
Schedule BCMS internal audits so that they involve a variety of individuals as well as activities (remembering to also schedule the audits based on the results of the risk assessments of the organisation's activities).	Communicate the results of internal audits throughout the business. Depending on the organisation's culture, this could be by high level summary or a more detailed scorecard. In any event, it should focus on the positive outcomes as well as identify improvements.
By implementing an internal audit schedule, which is spread throughout the year, the auditor/s will be better equipped to maintain and develop their competency and experience levels. Allocate ownership of the auditors' competency requirements to someone specific and make sure that periodic reviews are undertaken to ensure that the internal audits are delivering the level of scrutiny that is required by the business.	Revert to the organisation's BC policy and objectives throughout the year. Consider whether these objectives are being met and whether the allocated resources continue to carry out their BC responsibilities to the required, predetermined levels. Offer refresher training where necessary.
When the time comes to review individual BIA's, try and involve as many staff as is practicable. Individuals' working knowledge is invaluable and the benefit of asking for someone's input will help bring them into the process, especially where they see the results of their work being used by the business.	Consider communicating the results of periodical BIA reviews throughout the organisation. This will help to clarify where the business has changed or identify new risks that it faces.
Encourage individuals to contribute to any company improvement system you operate. This may be particularly relevant if they have recently been involved with an exercise, test, self assessment or internal audit.	Periodically, communicate the improvements that the organisation has chosen to implement as a result of reviewing staff contributions to these logs. Other improvements identified from other means should also be included.

Self evaluation of BCM arrangements

In order for you to be in control of your BC procedures and arrangements, you should implement a self evaluation programme. This will enable you to demonstrate, both internally and to external interested parties, that your BC arrangements remain fit for purpose.

A typical self evaluation process could include:

- Detailed reviews of key BC components such as the BIA, risk assessment process or validity of plans;

- Detailed analysis of outcomes from exercises and tests and the treatment of adverse trends;

- Discussions with members of staff about their perception of performance and effectiveness against established BC objectives;

- The issue of a survey or questionnaire to groups of staff or the entire organ-isation, seeking feedback and evidence of individual awareness of the BCM arrangements;

- Staff or team interviews to compare the perceptions of management to that of staff.

Having identified your preferred method, you should then:

- Determine the frequency of self evaluation;

- Determine what the objectives of the evaluation exercise are;

- Determine who will form the evaluation team;

- Agree the method and implement;

- Assess the feedback/information received;

- Obtain a consensus by the assessment team based on the feedback;

- Produce a suitable feedback report;

- Identify an appropriate action plan and incorporate it into the ongoing development of BC arrangements, objectives and organisational strategy, as appropriate.

However you choose to evaluate the effectiveness of your BC arrangements, and whatever the frequency, the most important point is to make the business aware of what you are doing and the results. By undertaking this course, you will retain people's attention and keep them progressing in the same direction as you.

TOP TIP

Maintaining momentum requires creative thinking and a good understanding of your organisation's culture. Select your preferred options carefully and make it fun.

ACTION SHEET

Note down here how you might maintain the momentum of your BCM arrangements.

Method	Participants

SUMMARY

(1) Think carefully about what you want from your certification body and prepare a shortlist to select your preferred supplier from.

(2) Understand each phase of the audit process and prepare accordingly. Consider the benefits of a gap analysis and how far in advance of the stage 1 you should undertake this.

(3) Do not rush into the stage 2 initial audit. Make sure your BCMS is sufficiently embedded into the organisation in order to be able to demonstrate its effectiveness.

(4) Be prepared for each audit and gather your evidence in a way that you will find easy to present to the auditor.

(5) Depersonalise the audit process to help staff cope with being audited.

(6) Involve staff in the development of your BCMS and manage their expectations during the audit process.

(7) Validate the effectiveness of your BCMS through a programme of self assessments. Identify ways to keep assessments interesting and worthwhile.

(8) Appoint local BCM champions to promote 'best BCM practice' where appropriate.

APPENDIX A

EVALUATING THE PERFORMANCE OF YOUR BUSINESS CONTINUITY MANAGEMENT SYSTEM

In order to get the most out of your business continuity management system you will need to review its operation against pre determined objectives and measures, confirm whether it is performing in such a way so as to meet these, and identify any problems that need further investigation and/or action along the way. In other words, you will carry out a full cycle of **Plan Do Check Act** in this exercise alone. This is summarised in Figure A.1.

Figure A.1 Plan Do Check Act model

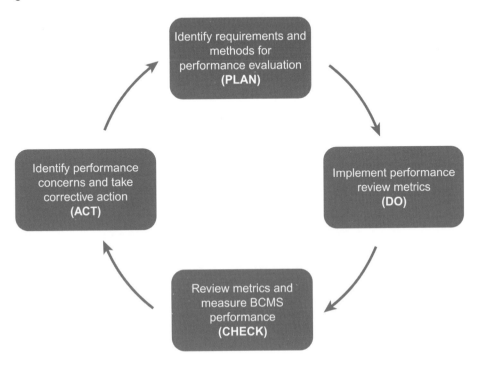

By applying the PDCA model as shown in Figure A.1, BCMS performance evaluation and effectiveness can be assessed in a straight forward and systematic way.

By completing the stages detailed in the following checklist you will have determined:

(1) How to select the most appropriate metrics for your organisation;

(2) What to do with the measurement results;

(3) How to use the results to improve your BCMS.

Why collate performance metrics?

- To understand, through objective evidence, how the BCMS is performing against pre determined objectives and measures.

- To manage expectations and set benchmarks for key performance areas.

- To make the BCMS a meaningful and useful tool.

- To enable root cause analysis of problem areas.

- To initiate regular and systematic measurement, monitoring and evaluation systems for the BCMS.

- To measure and verify BCMS compliance against ISO 22301 requirements.

- To involve top management in performance analysis and obtain their engagement in corrective actions.

- To drive improvement in performance related areas.

- By identifying and applying pre determined metrics you will reduce double counting and over analysis of information.

How to select the most appropriate metrics for your organisation

Considerations	Your response/actions
1. Review your BCMS objectives and identify the activities which will provide the best evaluation of performance.	
2. Identify the processes and procedures in place to protect prioritised activities. How are these currently monitored or reviewed? Can this information be used to support BCMS performance metrics?	
3. ISO 22301 compliance requirements provide numerous opportunities to assess BCMS performance. These include: ● Internal and external audit results ● Exercise and test results ● Invocation outcomes ● Management reviews ● BIA and other BCM reviews.	
4. Split metrics between BCM performance and BCMS compliance outputs and be clear about your objectives for each.	
5. Consider both qualitative and quantitative measures of performance. An example of each might be: Qualitative = supplier performance and relationship following involvement in exercise(s) Quantitative = frequency and number of near misses following BCMS implementation (industry sector driven).	
6. Consider performance by those outside the organisation on whom your organisation is dependent. This might include: ● Outsourced partners ● Suppliers ● Contractors ● Mutual aid providers	
7. Consider legal, regulatory or contractual requirements and set up review process to assess breaches and any resulting penalties	

What to do with the measurement results

Considerations	Your response/actions
1. Analysis should highlight both success and areas for improvement.	
2. Categorise performance results for easier reporting. Categories might include: • Activity related • Business strategy related • Overall business performance related • Customer satisfaction • Financial impact • Compliance related.	
3. Enter performance information into a centrally managed tool (this could be as simple as a spreadsheet), review it and draw conclusions from it.	
4. Once reviewed, submit your analysis and conclusions to top management (possibly as part of the management review process). Also, disseminate findings to those who are able to affect change and improvement.	
5. Compare information between periods and identify trends. Report findings as necessary.	

How to use the results to improve your BCMS

Considerations	Your response/actions
1. Identify areas for change (this may be a need for cultural change).	
2. Identify requirements for new procedures.	
3. Identify potential new risks.	
4. Use performance results to develop staff awareness and involvement of BCMS.	
5. React promptly to trends.	
6. Use the results to confirm (or not) that the business continuity policy and objectives are still appropriate and being met.	
7. Involve staff with decision making where appropriate and embed a culture of accepting change and improvement.	
8. Perform periodic reviews to check whether the changes implemented have been effective (the results may prompt the start of the PDCA cycle again).	

APPENDIX B

ISO 22301 SELF ASSESSMENT CHECKLIST

The purpose of this self assessment checklist is to help you identify whether your BCMS has addressed the fundamental requirements of ISO 22301. It does not ask you to confirm compliance to every clause in the standard, but does provide you with a reasonable assessment of the current status of your business continuity management system, identifies where specific evidence is located and what, if any, further action is required.

Requirement	Self assessment question	Response	Evidence (type/location)	Further action required	By whom/ when
Context of the Organisation **ISO 22301** **Clause 4**	Have you **documented** the organisation's products, services, functions and activities?				
	Who are the organisation's **interested parties** and why?	1. 2. 3. 4. 5. 6. 7. 8. 9. 10.			
	What has been considered when establishing the **needs and requirements** of the organisation and interested parties?				

(Continued)

Requirement	Self assessment question	Response	Evidence (type/location)	Further action required	By whom/ when
Context of the Organisation	What might be the **impact** on these requirements in the event of a disruption?				
	What is the organisation's **risk appetite** and on what basis has this been determined?				
	Have **legal and regulatory** requirements of the organisation and interested parties been considered and documented?				
	Has the **scope** of the BCMS been defined and any exclusions identified?				
	Does the BCMS scope include products and services and related activities? How is it **communicated**?				
	Has the business continuity management system been established in line with the requirements of the standard, following the **PDCA cycle**?				
Leadership **ISO 22301** **Clause 5**	In what ways does **top management** proactively support the BCMS?	1. 2. 3.			
	Is there a clear **link** between the organisation's business strategy and the BCMS?				

(Continued)

Requirement	Self assessment question	Response	Evidence (type/location)	Further action required	By whom/ when
Leadership	a) How does top management ensure that suitable BCM **resource** is available and;	a)			
	b) how is **authority** assigned and communicated to staff?	b)			
Planning **ISO 22301** **Clause 6**	Has the organisation identified:				
	a) **risks** which might prevent it from achieving the objectives of the BCMS and;	a)			
	b) **opportunities** which could lead to preventing problems and BCMS improvement.	b)			
	Have business continuity (BC) **objectives** been established?				
	Are BC objectives clear, measurable and aligned to the BC Policy?				
	Have BC objectives been communicated to those concerned?				
	How is performance against objectives measured and evaluated?				

(Continued)

Requirement	Self assessment question	Response	Evidence (type/location)	Further action required	By whom/ when
Support **ISO 22301** **Clause 7**	On what basis was BCMS **resource** determined?				
	a) What method has been used to determine appropriate **competencies** for each BCMS role and;	a)			
	b) Is there a process for tracking achievement and maintenance of such competencies?	b)			
	Is everyone employed or contracted by the organisation aware of the BC policy and BCMS and the part they play in it? How is this communicated and how do you ascertain that this has been **understood** by individuals?				
	How does the organisation plan its BCMS communications, both internally and to interested parties? How does it know if these are **effective**? a) During business as usual? b) During and after an incident?	a) b)			
	Has the organisation documented its BCMS in accordance with ISO 22301 requirements? How is this presented and made available?				

(Continued)

Requirement	Self assessment question	Response	Evidence (type/location)	Further action required	By whom/ when
Support	What additional **information** has the organisation determined is appropriate to ensure an effective BCMS?				
	a) Is BCMS **documentation** appropriately identified, accessible, stored and maintained;	a)			
	b) how is this evidenced and;	b)			
	c) is it appropriate to the size and complexity of the organisation?	c)			
Operation ISO 22301 Clause 8	What methods are used to monitor and **control** activities that are contracted out and outsourced?				
	a) Is there a documented **business impact analysis** which identifies the activities that support the provision of products and services,	a)			
	b) considers impacts over time if these activities are not performed,	b)			
	c) sets prioritised timeframes for the resumption of these activities to a minimum level,	c)			
	(d) identifies supporting resources and dependencies for these activities.	(d)			

(Continued)

Requirement	Self assessment question	Response	Evidence (type/location)	Further action required	By whom/when
Operation	Is there a documented **risk assessment** process which supports the analysis of risks and applies appropriate treatments?				
	Have **BC strategies** been identified which reflect the findings from the BIA and risk assessment?				
	Have a broad range of **resources** been identified which will enable BC strategies to be implemented when required? What are they?				
	Have **documented procedures** been established to manage a disruptive incident and maintain prioritised activities in line with the BIA?				

(Continued)

Requirement	Self assessment question	Response	Evidence (type/location)	Further action required	By whom/ when
Operation	a) Has a **documented procedure** been produced which covers the management responsibilities required to respond to an incident?	a)			
	b) Does this procedure include **responsibility** for invocation, communication with interested parties, assessing the extent of the incident and invoking an appropriate BC response?	b)			
	Is there a **communications procedure** which includes information to be provided, when, by whom and to whom?				
	Are there **BC plans** designed to identify invocation requirements, prioritised procedures, resource requirements and defined roles and responsibilities?				
	Has the organisation identified how it will **restore** activities from their temporary nature in order to support normal business requirements?				

(Continued)

Requirement	Self assessment question	Response	Evidence (type/location)	Further action required	By whom/ when
Operation	Has a schedule of **exercises and tests** been developed which, taken together, will validate all BCM arrangements over time?				
	Have exercises and tests been carried out and, if so, do they demonstrate a variety of methods by which to assess the **effectiveness** of the BCMS?				
	Are the **results** of exercises and tests reviewed in order to identify ways of improving BCM arrangements?				
Performance Evaluation ISO 22301 Clause 9	How has the organisation determined what needs to be **measured**, by what means, the frequency, and when this information will be analysed?				
	Is there a process to follow when **adverse trends** are identified in order to prevent nonconformities from occurring?				

(Continued)

Requirement	Self assessment question	Response	Evidence (type/location)	Further action required	By whom/ when
Performance Evaluation	What methods exist to evaluate the **effectiveness** of BCM processes and procedures?				
	Has a programme of **internal audits** been developed with a reasoned approach to scheduling evident?				
	Have auditors been selected based on pre determined **competencies** and impartiality to the scope of each audit?				
	Is there a schedule of **management reviews** and is it under way? When was the last meeting held, and was top management well represented?				
	Have **minutes** been prepared following management reviews and do they include allocated actions and a method of following these up?				
Improvement **ISO 22301** **Clause 10**	a) By what method do you record nonconformities? b) By what method do you review and evaluate these nonconformities?	a) b)			
	How do you plan to improve your BCMS on a continual basis? Where might evidence of your methods be found?				

111

REFERENCES

BS 25999-1:2006 (2006), *Business Continuity Management – Code of Practice*, BSI, London.

BS 25999-2:2007 (2007), *Business Continuity Management – Specification*, BSI, London.

BS EN ISO 19011:2011 (2011), *Guidelines for Auditing Management Systems*, BSI, London.

BS EN ISO/IEC 17021:2011 (2011), *Conformity Assessment – Requirements for Bodies Providing Audit and Certification of Management Systems*, BSI, London.

BS EN ISO 9000:2005 (2005), *Quality Management Systems. Fundamentals and Vocabulary*, BSI, London.

ISO DIS 22313:2011 (2011), *Societal Security - Business Continuity Management Systems – Guidance*, BSI, London.

ISO FDIS 22301:2012 and BS ISO 22301:2012 (2012), *Societal Security – Business Continuity Management Systems – Requirements*, BSI, London.

ISO 22300:2012 (2012) *Societal Security – Terminology*, BSI, London.

PAS 99:2006 (2006), *Specification of Common Management System Requirements as a Framework for Integration*, BSI, London.

PD 25111:2010 (2010), *BCM Guidance on Human Aspects of Business Continuity*, BSI, London.

PD 25666:2010 (2010), *BCM Guidance on Exercising and Testing for Continuity and Contingency Programmes*, BSI, London.

PD 25222:2011 (2011), *BCM Guidance on Supply Chain Continuity*, BSI, London.

The Business Continuity Institute (2010), *BCI Good Practice Guidelines 2010*, BCI, Caversham.

SOURCES OF FURTHER INFORMATION

Perpetual Solutions Limited
www.pslinfo.co.uk
01844 298894

The Business Continuity Institute
www.thebci.org
0118 947 8215

International Register of Certificated Auditors (IRCA)
www.irca.org
020 7245 6833

The United Kingdom Accreditation Service (UKAS)
www.ukas.com
020 89178400

INDEX

114